**Envisioning
Better
Cities**

Envisioning Better Cities

A Global Tour of Good Ideas

Patricia Chase and Nancy K. Rivenburgh, PhD

ORO

ORO Editions
Publishers of Architecture, Art, and Design
Gordon Goff: Publisher

www.oroeditions.com
info@oroeditions.com

Published by ORO Editions

Text: Patricia Chase and Nancy K. Rivenburgh
Project Coordinator: Kirby Anderson

Book Design: Pablo Mandel
Typeset in Minion Pro and URW Geometric

10 9 8 7 6 5 4 3 2 1 First Edition

Library of Congress data available upon request.
World Rights: Available

ISBN: 978-1-941806-54-8

Color Separations and Printing: ORO Group Ltd.
Printed in China.

International Distribution: www.oroeditions.com/distribution

ORO Editions makes a continuous effort to minimize the overall carbon footprint of its publications. As part of this goal, ORO Editions, in association with Global ReLeaf, arranges to plant trees to replace those used in the manufacturing of the paper produced for its books. Global ReLeaf is an international campaign run by American Forests, one of the world's oldest nonprofit conservation organizations. Global ReLeaf is American Forests' education and action program that helps individuals, organizations, agencies, and corporations improve the local and global environment by planting and caring for trees.

Contents

1/

Introduction

Take an Inspired Global Tour

You are about to embark on an exciting tour of useful, feasible, and novel ideas for making cities more livable and sustainable. You will visit cities of all sizes and locations to see what people are doing to improve their communities.

Cities around the world face common global challenges: climate change, population growth, income and health disparities, natural resource degradation, pollution, and social isolation. Each city also faces its own set of local challenges. This might include budget pressures, NIMBYism, provincialism, outdated regulatory structures, lack of political courage, or public resistance to change. We trust that you know these challenges as well. So, rather than elaborating on the negatives, the purpose of *Envisioning Better Cities: A Global Tour of Good Ideas* is to promote positive change. We focus on successful steps that people around the world have *already* taken in hopes of inspiring other change agents, like you.

Several key themes guide this journey:

It's all about people
Cities are for people to live, work, socialize, and play. The best cities inspire a sense of belonging, pride, joy, equity, and spirit of cooperation. They make

decisions that prioritize public health, quality of life, and improvements to their environmental ecosystem. No matter their size, the best cities share the wealth by giving *everyone* access and opportunity to enjoy city spaces, services, and amenities without feeling unwelcome or inferior. We try to express these beliefs in chapter headings, as well as through the examples they contain: Inviting People, Inspiring People, Connecting People, Communicating with People, Moving People, and Supporting People. We argue that cities must strive to do *all* these tasks well.

Every city has tremendous assets

Most cities have much to work with. Unique natural environments. A history that includes great stories, old buildings and industries, and meaningful events. A personality and cultural heritage. Public spaces. Some of these features may now feel lost, covered with concrete or perhaps have become bland or forgotten. But much can happen by reinvigorating, repurposing, recovering, and retrofitting what is already there. Cities can refresh places, programs, and policies in authentic, yet forward-looking ways. Cities also have the most important asset of all: people. People with diverse talents, energy, compassion, and a desire for their city to be distinctive and alive.

Good ideas travel

This book visits over a hundred cities around the world. One thing we have learned is that cities of similar sizes tend to share similar challenges. And, while no city does everything right, so many cities do something clever or exciting that makes living there better. For this reason, it's important to look beyond one's own city or culture for ideas, best practices, and different perspectives; to learn about what others have successfully done, then to adapt, combine, and improve on those ideas is the definition of creative problem solving – and a terrific formula for making better cities.

Small is big

This book offers ideas of all sizes. Some of the best ideas that we showcase involve very little money, relying on creativity and energy. Hosting a mural contest. Opening a street for kid's play. Planting trees. Others, yes, involve millions of dollars in capital expenditure for infrastructure, relying on

2/

Inviting People

A livable and sustainable city needs people of all ages and means who participate in city life for more than work. In the best cities, people enjoy exploring the streets, relaxing with their family at a park, or checking out this week's festival. They are proud of where they live.

Urban designer Jan Gehl believes that a city must invite people to enjoy its public spaces. In his book *Cities for People*, he writes that too much urban planning focuses on just moving people through the city. Instead, cities should entice people to linger, explore, and engage. According to Gehl, people will do what you invite them to do. If you build more roads, they will drive more. If you create more pedestrian and bicycles pathways, they will walk and bike more. If you provide more inviting public spaces, people will visit and enjoy them.

We start this book's global tour by insisting that inviting people is a prerequisite to more involved types of engagement covered in subsequent chapters, such as promoting inspiration, connection, and communication among people. In crafting attractive urban invitations it is useful to consider three key ideas: atmosphere, activity, and inclusivity.

Set the Atmosphere

What entices people to want to stay in a neighborhood or city? Here, we're not talking about the housing, businesses, and services that are essential

2-1　　　　　　　　　　2-2

to daily life. We're talking about the personal experience, or sensation, of just being in a place: the atmosphere. One way to identify the features that contribute to a positive atmosphere is to ask, "What do people avoid?" People feel insignificant in places that are too large and impersonal. They avoid places where traffic moves too fast and loud. They circumvent areas that seem dangerous or confusing or bland. This tells us that human-oriented scale, safety, comfort, and sensory appeal comprise the basic, and necessary, conditions for an inviting atmosphere.

Human Scale

Who doesn't like to wander along the narrow streets of old cities? These ancient, irregular streets often leading to town squares, cathedrals, or temples emerged from the "beaten path," the most natural route considering environmental factors such as topography and protection from the elements. The public spaces of these old towns embodied a sense of intimacy, informality, and welcome.

One can see human scale nestled in the heart of Shanghai's Old Town where the narrow streets of Yu Garden and Bazaar weave among old-style Chinese buildings adjacent to a classical Chinese garden. Small shops sell spices, silk pajamas, and a wealth of sensory interest (2-1). In the same way, the outdoor cafes dotting so many of the narrow streets of Europe's traditional cities, like this street in the Trastevere neighborhood of Rome (2-2), epitomize the attraction of human scale. For centuries, such places invited people to slow down, perhaps have a coffee, and stay awhile.

As the mode of travel evolved from walking to horses and carriages and then to motor vehicles, city designs imposed straight grids on the landscape.

2-3

2-6

2-4

2-5

2-7

From a practical perspective, the grid infrastructure made sense. However, from an atmosphere perspective, grid layouts have made cities less friendly. But that doesn't need to be the case. There are many ways to create a sense of enclosure within larger, more formal patterns. Inviting cities know how to make big seem small.

One of the ways that cities, already dominated by grid layouts, try to recapture a sense of human scale is to reclaim alleys that over time have become unfriendly and unattractive.

A great example is in Melbourne, Australia. Melbourne's central business district laneways date back to the Victorian era when they bustled with activity as service lanes or shopping arcades. Over the decades these laneways became dirty and dangerous (2-3). Starting in the mid 1980s the city began a concerted effort to take back their laneways turning some into stylish pedestrian restaurant and shopping alleys and others into creative canvases for urban art (now a significant tourist attraction). Part of this process included improving lighting, paving, and connectivity within this pedestrian network. The city also limited vehicular access and allowed tenants along the laneways, whether shops or restaurants, to open their businesses out into the lanes (2-4). The revitalization of its historic laneways

2-8

is just one reason why Melbourne is one of the most livable cities in the world.

Several North American cities are following Melbourne's lead. Projects in Chicago, Seattle, Montreal, Los Angeles, and Washington, D.C. are reclaiming service lanes, alleys, or back streets behind houses into human-scale streets and green pathways. The potential is great. Just consider that Chicago has 1,900 miles of alleyways. In Chicago's Green Alley Program, the city is not only renovating alleys for people, but replacing many asphalt surfaces with semi-permeable surfaces to allow for better filtering of stormwater run-off: a good idea with multiple benefits.

If the widths of streets cannot change, then techniques such as tree canopies can provide a sense of human scale and intimacy, as shown here in Portland, Oregon (2-5). People enjoy the multiple benefits of intimacy, greenery, protection from weather, and cleaner air. Urban features such as pocket parks and street cafes under awnings also create more human-scale enclosures within a larger street or plaza area. Even something as simple as stringing lights across the street and putting out some picnic tables creates a sense of enclosure. The residents, shops, and restaurants on Portland, Oregon's SW Ankeny St. decided to try just that, creating a cozy one-block area for gathering in the evening (2-6).

Contemporary urban planners are incorporating human scale into the design of new neighborhoods and districts. One example is the design of the Bo01 section of Västra Hamnen (Western Harbour) in Malmo, Sweden. Taller commercial and residential buildings face the Oresund Sound acting like a city wall to protect the inner neighborhood from the intense sea winds (2-7). Inside, one- and two-story buildings connect through a series of courtyards and narrow, meandering streets in this mixed-use neighborhood (2-8). The design is a nod to the medieval street designs of Malmo's past still found in the historic center of the city.

To design new construction with narrower streets requires some adaptations. Essential vehicles such as fire trucks, must be narrower. Other innovations can eliminate the need for large trucks. In the Stockholm

2-9

2-10

neighborhood of Hammarby Sjöstad an underground street vacuum system, powered by electric generators, collects recycling and garbage. These receptacles, which are at street level or located within residential buildings and offices, connect to pipes that run three to six feet beneath the ground to the transfer station (2-9). From the transfer station, trucks take the materials to their appropriate destinations. Not having garbage cans eliminates odors and the pests that garbage attracts. Although capital expenditures are high in installing the receptacles and pipes, operational costs are very low as fewer workers are needed.

Safety

A city cannot be inviting if it does not feel safe. While it may seem naïve to think that a high crime city or neighborhood will become safer without tackling underlying economic or social inequities, one can still challenge some assumptions about what urban features "promote" safety. For example, studies reveal that a neighborhood full of high fences, bars, and surveillance cameras do not make a city feel safer. They foster an atmosphere of fear, separation, and barriers.

This street scene in La Boca, Buenos Aires boasts multiple features of a safe and inviting atmosphere (2-10). There are eyes on the street. People can watch other people from tables and balconies or strolling along the sidewalk. There are shops, a sense of a life, and the buzz of social interaction day and evening. Both eight- and 80-year-olds would feel comfortable here.

Places such as this lovely plaza in Leipzig, Germany (2-11) remind us of the importance of good lighting for people to feel not only safer, but eager to take an evening stroll. Not all light is created equal. Choices of

2-11

2-12

direction, hue, and range exist. Ideally, the light cast is soft and friendly, the fixtures interesting, and effect allows for accurate viewing of colors and people without glare. Switching to LED lights allows light intensity and quality to be adjusted for specific circumstances. In many cases, improved lighting above streets, on buildings, on street signs, and integrated into sidewalk pavers becomes a key ingredient in efforts to revitalize degraded or old neighborhoods.

When people lack information and feel uncertain about their situation, they experience a corresponding sense of anxiety. This can manifest itself as a mild sense of excitement about being in new surroundings or as fear or intimidation. Cities that have clear wayfinding signage, easy-to-identify landmarks, and logical pathways that connect key destinations provide a greater sense of certainty and security for visitors and residents, while actively promoting urban exploration.

The "Legible London" initiative is a good example of a citywide effort to transform a confusing and intimidating city to feel inviting and safe to walk around (2-12). A 2006 study revealed a significant list of obstacles that prevented people from feeling confident walking around London – not the least of which was the discovery of 32 distinct wayfinding systems within the city, each using different types of signs, formats, and logic. The study also discovered that when people lacked directions, they took the subway system (the Tube) even if travel would be quicker by foot. Guided by the design principle, "Don't make me think," Legible London designers

2-13

2-14

2-15

2-16

2-17

2-18

developed a more intuitive, clear, and consistent wayfinding system involving place signs, street signs, directional and en route signs, information panels, trail markers, lighting, and a host of complementary resources such as coordinated pocket maps and on-line or on-demand information accessible by smartphone. The system works seamlessly across all modes of travel. This sign along the River Thames employs some helpful wayfinding techniques such as: "heads-up mapping" where the top of the map is the direction ahead (not north); a circle to identify sites within a five- to 15-minute walking radius; a "You are Here" icon; and key destinations and facilities (e.g., museums, parks, restrooms, transit), along with walking times to them.

Sometimes the unexpected can promote safer streets. Mary Soderstrom in her book *The Walkable City: From Haussmann's Boulevards to Jane Jacobs' Streets and Beyond* found that city housing that allows people to have pets puts more people on the streets, day and night, walking their dogs – as shown here in New York City (2-13). This, in turn, promotes safer areas as well as contributes to personal health and community building as residents take daily walks and get to know each other through their pets.

Safety also relates to protection against accidents and injury. We know, for example, that slow is safer. Victor Dover and John Massengale in their book *Street Design: The Secret to Great Cities and Towns* put a strong emphasis on slowing cars down to 20 miles per hour or less in urban settings and neighborhoods. They advocate techniques such as putting sculptures, plantings, or fountains in the middle of the road to force drivers to slow down and be more cognizant of their surroundings.

The condition of sidewalks, the safety of pedestrian crossings, the mitigation of hazards for bicyclists, clearing snow and ice for pedestrians, and more, also contribute to safer places. In Enschede, Netherlands, the design of this metal rain gutter prevents a bicycle wheel from falling into it (2-14). Other rain gutters might run perpendicular to the flow of bike traffic for the same reason.

Comfort

What's comfortable in a city? Comfort is clean air, no noxious smells, and noise levels that allow for conversation. Benches, low walls, or chairs offer plenty of places to sit or rest. Well placed heat lamps, awnings, umbrellas, and lighting shown here at a cafe in San Francisco (2-15) or these trees in a pocket park in Stockholm (2-16) protect people from the elements. During the hottest months of the year in Malaga, Spain, the city places see-through banners over the primary outdoor pedestrian mall to provide relief from the sun without losing a sense of being outside (2-17).

Inviting cities offer an atmosphere that is alive with people. However, it's also important to have public spaces for escape. People need enclaves of peace, quiet, and greenery tucked away from the bustle of city streets. Here, men in Baku, Azerbaijan play chess in a city park away from car fumes and noise (2-18).

Sensory Appeal

Walking around an inviting city is an experience that engages all five senses in stimulating and uplifting ways: sight, sound, touch, smell, and taste. Some cities boast a geographic setting that naturally delights the senses with features such as the smell and taste of ocean air, views of snow-capped mountains, or the ripple of a river running through the city center.

Other cities create a sensory atmosphere through the integration of nature, design, and activity.

Jan Gehl is well known for his concept of "soft edges": streetscapes that are dynamic, textured, and detailed at eye level. For example, Gehl would suggest that this street should close not for the construction, but for its dull stretch of hard-edged, horizontal lines (2-19). By contrast, streetscapes with soft edges appeal to the senses. He advocates for one- and two-story vertically oriented buildings with doorways every few feet, and windows looking onto the street – ideally punctuated with visually appealing detail. For example, soft edges provide a sensory experience along this street in Cartagena, Colombia (2-20).

The sensuous light cast by this giant, art replica of a table lamp in Lille Torv (Small Square) in Malmo, Sweden warms the dark, cold night (2-21). In a different type of sensory experience, the fountain lights of Cheonggyecheon Plaza in Seoul, Korea add energy to an evening out (2-22).

Equally important are the subtle patterns and spatial rhythms that define or detail an urban setting. We are not always conscious of these sensory inputs, but experience them nonetheless. For example, people are drawn to ordered contrasts: repeated shapes with contrasting color or textures. These painted row houses in Washington, D.C. (2-23) or the artful display of goods in this Istanbul market (2-24) are examples. In a similar way, the complex architectural patterns in the Liege, Belgium train station (2-25) or a simple paver design at the base of a tree in Burlington, Vermont (2-26) appeal to our senses.

We love cities that abound in tantalizing textures and smells. Maybe it is wisteria climbing a building in Brussels (2-27), rough rock walls contrasting with multi-colored fruit in Jerusalem (2-28), or this Hanoi marketplace of seafood and spices (2-29). Or, maybe it's the sounds of street musicians in Vienna (2-30), horse-drawn carriages in Bruges (2-31), or the diffuse chatter of an open-air café. Historically, in Europe and older cities of the United States, smells and sounds functioned like signposts in a city. Bakeries guided people into the town center with smells of freshly baked bread and sweet jam-filled goodies. In Japan or Korea, incense leads the way to cherished temples. In contemporary urban planning and retrofitting, attention to sounds and smells can enhance neighborhood

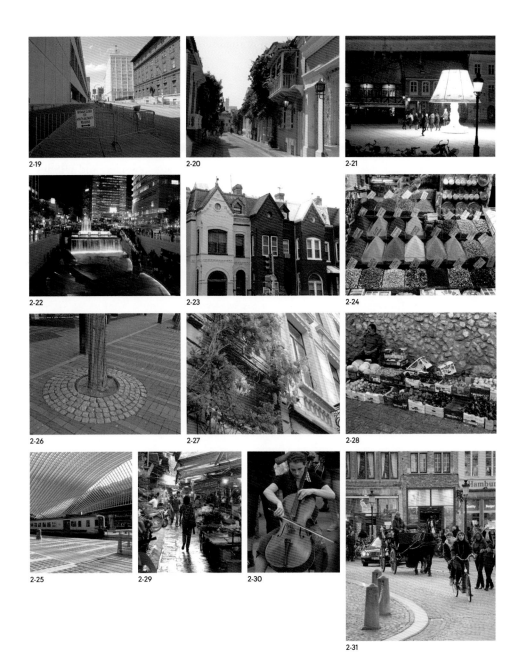

2-19

2-20

2-21

2-22

2-23

2-24

2-26

2-27

2-28

2-25

2-29

2-30

2-31

19

identity. The intent might be to associate floral scents with a quiet park or to welcome people, through alluring aromas, to a restaurant district.

Promote Activity

Jan Gehl offers another truism: "Where nothing happens, nothing happens." To encourage people to linger and enjoy the city, he promotes "stay" activities. Distinct from daily essentials of shopping and working, stay activities might include reading a book in the park, strolling with friends, playing active sports, attending a festival, or hanging out to people watch. Inviting cities promote activities that are planned, spontaneous, free, frequent, healthy, and accessible.

Planned and spontaneous

In addition to paid entertainment and events for public consumption, such as concerts, movie theaters, sports events, dance clubs, and museums, the most inviting cities allow for plenty of *planned* activities in public spaces. To accomplish this, cities need to provide the infrastructure that allows for a diversity of events, from this street festival in Kuala Lumpur, Malaysia to book fairs to kite contests (2-32). To enliven spaces, the organization Project for Public Spaces (PPS) recommends clustering activities to create a destination. PPS advocates locating these "activated" public spaces where they can serve multiple communities and include activities that celebrate diverse cultures.

Cities should also allow for *spontaneous* activities in public spaces, such this street performer in Havana, Cuba (2-33). Cities that encourage these "informal entrepreneurs" realize many benefits. Street performers (buskers) add vibrancy, surprise, and delight to urban life. They also make an area feel safer. It is a way for young musicians and magicians to practice in front of a live audience. On the audience side, people who might not ordinarily attend a concert can expand their musical horizons.

Beyond the entertainment and engagement value, allowing informal entrepreneurs supports a rapidly growing sector of urban citizen around the world. According to the Organization for Economic Co-operation and Development, today more than half the workers of the world (1.8 billion people) participate in the informal economy – that is, they live "off the

2-32 2-33 2-34

2-35 2-36

books." And that figure is growing. UN Habitat, in its Global Report on Human Settlements, advocates for more lenient policies and creative solutions for allowing buskers, waste pickers, market sellers, and street traders to be a vibrant and inviting part of city life. Street performers are also free entertainment (well, maybe add a tip to the hat).

Free and frequent

Cities benefit from *free* and *frequent* activities. Here, a big screen set up on La Rambla, Barcelona's tree-lined promenade, captivates pedestrians who stop to enjoy an opera performance (2-34). Also, on Saturday or Sundays throughout the summer months anyone can dance the Sardana, the traditional dance of Catalonia in plazas such as Plaça de Sant Jaume, the square in front of the Catedral de Barcelona, as well as at smaller squares throughout the city (2-35). A growing number of cities around the world offer free summer movie-series in parks or other open-air locations as this one in Pittsburgh (2-36). A daily, weekly, or less frequent visitor should always expect something to be going on in public spaces that is new and different and free.

Healthy and accessible

Urban activities offer positive mental and physical health benefits. The "Healthy Cities" movement that started to gain academic and professional traction in the 1980s offers convincing evidence of the inextricable link between urban planning and public health. The sub-field of environmental health investigates how the design of urban settings can attract people to engage in healthier lifestyles through more daily walking and better access to recreational physical activity. Both community design and the programming of *healthy* and *accessible* activities can help alleviate, rather than exacerbate, risk factors associated with sedentary lifestyles, obesity, heart disease, and asthma.

The Leichhardt Park (Sydney) fitness area has a bold sign stating, "Welcome! You're Never Too Old to Play" (2-37). To encourage people—of all ages—to exercise more, cities such as Barcelona, New York, Santiago, Tel Aviv, and, shown here, Shanghai (2-38) place exercise stations on the sidewalk for people to spontaneously use on their way to their destination or to visit as part of a daily routine.

Healthy cities also provide spaces for a diverse selection of recreational activities and events, ranging from scheduled exercise such as Zumba classes in Oaxaca's Zócalo (public square) or tai chi in a Beijing park (2-39), to hosting running or biking events, to providing facilities for skateboarding, swimming, ball games, table tennis, outdoor dancing, or ice skating.

Over the past three decades, expensive cities such as Paris, London, Copenhagen, and San Francisco have tried to become more fun places to live by offering affordable activities amidst the pricey restaurants. Residents can play ping pong in Paris (2-40) or waterski in Copenhagen. These teenagers, who themselves have energy to burn, don't mind the industrial backdrop because Copenhagen's contemporary waste-to-energy plants are non-polluting (2-41).

Mixed-use neighborhoods promote activity

While it comes as little surprise that having nearby parks, trails, and recreation facilities contributes to more recreational activity, mixed-use neighborhoods also promote activity and increase health. Research reveals that residents of neighborhoods that have a central core of diverse shops walk almost three times more than those who must shop along the kind of major arterial roadways that dominate most U.S. cities. This finding is true regardless of economic or demographic characteristics of the people or place. This, of course, is not news for Europeans where many walkable, mixed-use areas exist such as the Friedrichshain neighborhood in Berlin (2-42) or downtown Bitola in the Republic of Macedonia (2-43).

2-37

2-38

2-40

2-41

2-42

2-43

2-39

Invite Everyone

So, an inviting city is one with a positive *atmosphere* and plenty of *activities* to attract and engage people. But is everyone invited? A third key element of an inviting city is *inclusivity*. Everyone should be welcome in a city – large or small. Everyone should feel valued and respected.

To understand the benefits of inclusivity is to understand that healthy and sustainable habitats—whether we're talking about forests or cities—require diversity. Biologists and ecologists, of course, know this as scientific fact. And, increasingly, city planners and policymakers have embraced this principle as well: cities benefit from cultural, ethnic, religious, business, age, and socioeconomic diversity. In theory, being inclusive makes good sense. In practice, however, this means designing cities and neighborhoods to be more welcoming to more vulnerable populations. Groups of people that might have limits on personal mobility, such as older adults, or limits to their judgment, such as young children. Others might lack resources or education or language skills.

For a city to become more inclusive requires becoming more observant and thoughtful about designing spaces, programs, and policies for all users rather than the average user. Does this public square offer something for an eight-year-old to do? Could an 80-year-old sit in that same square in comfort? More broadly, can families raise their children in this city? Can residents remain in their neighborhoods as they age? Do people of all colors, nationalities, and religions feel accepted and included?

Cities in North America are not particularly inclusive. For example, research reveals that lower income residents experience unequal access to quality, clean, and aesthetically pleasing spaces. City layouts or poorly maintained sidewalks favor the agile and energetic and provide challenges, and significant risk of injury, for older adults. Many cities are not family friendly, lacking stimulating, safe, and affordable environments to raise children.

Age-Friendly Cities

Yet, making cities more inclusive is an urgent need. According to the U.S. Census Bureau, by 2050 over 83 million Americans will be 65 or older (nearly double the number from 2012). This trend is also true for most

2-44

other developed countries. For example, Germany, Italy, and Japan (2-44) already count 20% of their populations as 65 or older (the U.S. will reach that 20% figure by 2030). Projections suggest the number of Americans with a disability will rise from 51 to 80 million people by 2050. And, based on data from the U.S. census bureau, income inequality in the United States continues to increase, as does the cultural, ethnic, and religious makeup of our cities.

With urbanization and population aging as two major global trends, the World Health Organization (WHO) promotes guidelines for age-friendly cities based on focus group research with adults over 65 in countries around the world. The results reveal three overarching areas of concern: 1) safe passage, 2) places to go and be, and 3) feeling welcome. The good news is that urban features beneficial to seniors tend to benefit everyone.

Safe Passage. This concern is really a collection of issues related to the ability to move safely around one's neighborhood or city. It is common for older adults to experience a loss of muscle strength and increased stiffness as they age, slowing their movements and increasing their tendency to shuffle. This makes even small pedestrian obstacles more conducive to falling. In fact, the fear of falling is higher than the fear of crime for most elder adults. And, rightly so. One in every three people over 65 experiences a fall-related injury. To welcome seniors, age-friendly cities need to consider sidewalk width to allow elderly to avoid trees or vendors, to move at their own pace, and to accommodate wheelchairs. Cracked or uneven sidewalks need repair. Materials used for pedestrian ways should not become slippery when wet or have overly high curbs. Where curb ramps exist, they shouldn't be too steep or in poor repair. One successful strategy for areas with traditional cobblestone or decorative pavers is to insert a smooth paving strip wide enough to facilitate visitors with walkers or wheelchairs, as well as strollers and women in high heels. This example is on a pedestrian way in Potsdam, Germany (2-45).

Stairs in the city, without alternatives, can become a dangerous or physically challenging barrier to mobility for the elderly, the disabled, or parents with strollers (2-46). Seniors also need places to rest along the way to their destination as in this park in Lisbon (2-47).

How fast do you think this woman can cross the street (2-48)? Elders who feel rushed crossing the street get flustered, increasing the chance of a fall. In age-friendly cities there first needs to be enough street crossings, clearly marked. Ideally, the crosswalk offers both audio and visual cues to initiate the cross and enough time to complete it. One emerging technology is pedestrian user-friendly intelligent signals (PUFFIN). PUFFIN sensors detect slower pedestrians as they cross and automatically add time to the crossing signal. In addition, good street drainage is important. It is hard for seniors to jump over puddles! Other strategies include intersection "bulb-outs" to slow traffic and create shorter street crossings, mid-crossing "refuges" or medians (as this one in Washington, D.C., 2-49), raised cross-walks to the level of the curb, or early stop lines for cars – typically 15 feet before an intersection.

We also know that older adults and people with cognitive or physical liabilities can face challenges in finding their way. For example, a person with a walker focusing attention to obstacles on the sidewalk may more easily miss a directional sign. Seniors can get disoriented or lost more easily. Attention to the size of print on signs, providing good lighting for legibility, and combining words, symbols, color, and even textures to signal directions or transitions from sidewalk to street are helpful strategies. In a significant effort, Charlotte, North Carolina retrofitted dozens of streets to better accommodate seniors guided, in part, by the WHO guideline for wayfinding in age-friendly cities: "Write simple, short, with big letters."

While all communities urge people to take public transportation,

2-45　　　2-46　　　2-47

2-48　　　2-49　　　2-50

many seniors have no other option. Some basic age-friendly strategies can improve this experience. Public transportation needs to be affordable, reliable, frequent, clean, safe, and comfortable to ride and wait. These features, of course, benefit everyone. For older adults, access to buses, shuttles, or other transit needs to have ramps or elevated entrances, good lighting and seating at stops, elevators, or escalators. Here is a ramp for access to a tram in Poland (2-50). Directional information must be clear to read and understand. On board, seniors need priority seating and patient (and polite) drivers. Perhaps most important, does transit stop where seniors need to go, such as parks, banks, grocery stores, medical clinics, and libraries? Many cities offer micro-transit (van) options for door-to-door transport or senior discounts on taxi fares. Some even offer education programs for seniors in how to use public transport.

Places to go and be (comfortable). Older adults, as with anyone, want and need places to socialize and things to do. Age-friendly cities offer plenty of places outside of one's residence that are comfortable destinations for seniors. This might be cafes, small parks, libraries, or seating close to an ice cream vendor. Such places should be easy to get to, free or affordable, and welcoming. Urban anthropologist Phil Stafford recommends retrofit

2-51

2-52

2-53

strategies that create smaller "pocket" neighborhoods within larger neighborhoods. By altering road patterns, changing zoning, adding pedestrian only pathways, and bringing in satellite services (such as neighborhood health clinics), cities can help promote "aging in place" communities.

Seniors, as with everyone, enjoy green spaces that place them away from noise, odors, or car pollution. Public seating should be in places where seniors won't feel intimidated, yet can look at something interesting. These storefront benches in St. Jacobs, Ontario offer a good example of a setting welcoming to seniors (2-51). And comfort matters. Benches with backs and arms to aid getting up and down are helpful as is protection from weather – especially shade on a hot day. Notice how these Chilean seniors gravitate to the shade (2-52). Providing such respite from the sun in city spaces, whether using trees, umbrellas or awnings is critical.

Inviting People

Feeling Welcome. One of the most frequent complaints of seniors is that they don't feel welcome in their communities. To address this, New York City is a leader with its establishment of Aging Improvement Districts. Taking its cue from the World Health Organization, New York City launched its own Age-Friendly New York initiative. In 2010 a pilot project in East Harlem collected input from more that 200 community seniors in English, Spanish, and Cantonese about ways in which the city could better serve them. Results of that initiative have seen close to 60 neighborhood businesses provide more indoor and outdoor seating, and even separate lines, for seniors. The neighborhood now offers cleaner and more accessible public toilets, better access to laundry and other facilities, dedicated swim time for seniors at the neighborhood pool, large type for in-store signs, special bus trips to the farmer's market, and much more.

Parks and recreation programs that offer activities for seniors should allow for them to participate with a friend or caregiver, be during times convenient for older people, and promoted through channels that older adults use. One mistake is to offer too many seniors-only programs when, in fact, older adults often prefer intergenerational activities, if they feel comfortable and welcome. The Marion Intergenerational Garden is a community garden in Washington, D.C. with a mission to welcome all ages (2-53).

Most of the strategies for making cities more age-friendly also benefit the disabled, blind, or hard of hearing. In Kyoto-shi, Japan there are textured areas throughout the town to assist the blind. Dots signal a change (stairs, ramp, turn). Lines mean a straight path. Longer dots indicate a curve (2-54). This play area in Tamworth, Australia is welcoming to children in wheelchairs (2-55).

2-54   2-55

Family Friendly Cities

In the desire to attract young professionals and high-rise condo dwellers, cities miss out on the true heart of an inviting and sustainable city: families. Most downtowns are not attractive to families. Research shows that once children reach school age, families tend to move out of downtown – if they lived there in the first place. Traffic makes urban cores unsafe. There is a lack of schools. The commercial and entertainment focus is on adults. But families should be a key element of urban life. The benefits are many. Catering more to families supports a greater diversity of businesses. It puts the workforce closer to their jobs. It cuts down on commute time, which is good for the environment and allows parents to spend more time with their children, making for happier employees and people. Families engage with diverse social networks, care about safe and clean streets, and ideally raise children who will care about "their city." For residents without children, the presence of families conveys a sense of safety, fosters a neighborhood feel, and ideally brings a smile watching a child's joyful play.

From the children's perspective, living in a healthy and diverse city offers important and stimulating exposure to different types of people, situations, religions, businesses, and cultural resources such as the arts and libraries. Kids learn more about how the world works. They build important social skills. Inviting cities are also stimulating to a child's developing brain, offering a variety of textures, shapes, designs, colors, history, art, and spaces to provoke imagination, play, and exploration. Suzanne Crowhurst Lennard, founder and director of the International Making Cities Livable organization says that, "At its best, the public realm is an incomparable teacher of social skills and attitudes for children."

To attract families, more aspects of the built environment, as well as community programs, must support children's ability to learn and play within the city. For example, there should be plenty of city parks and opportunities for outdoor and street play. These kids enjoy a game of street hockey in Vancouver, British Columbia (2-56), while others splash in a fountain in Davis, California (2-57).

Play Streets is a program found in several cities that creates temporary space for young people to play. During regularly scheduled Play Street days and times, signs re-route traffic and open a local street to families

2-56   2-57   2-58

2-59

and children for play (2-58). Other programs, such as cicLAvia in Los Angeles offer opportunities to groom future urban cyclists. This excited three-year-old races along on a street that is car-free for this event (2-59).

To attract families to urban areas also requires quality schools and safe ways to walk and bike to them. It requires housing with three bedrooms affordable for a middle-class workforce – not just high-rise condos or micro-apartments for twenty-something professionals. The Ramona apartments, located in Portland's Pearl District, is part of that city's attempt to attract more families into the urban core. The apartment courtyard offers play spaces with plenty of seating for parents. Tricycles and strollers fit easily on wide walkways. The ground floor houses an elementary school. The Ramona's location offers easy walk, bike, and transit access to workplaces across the metro area (2-60).

Equitable Access

An inclusive and inviting city is multi-generational, multi-ethnic, multi-cultural, and mixed income. But in an increasing number of cities, mid- to

2-60

lower-income families and individuals cannot financially survive and are leaving the city for suburbs – in many cases breaking apart communities that have been in place for generations. Practically, what this means is a city's teachers, police officers, firefighters, and other municipal workers are unable to live in or near the neighborhoods where they work. It makes low-cost labor scarce for downtown businesses and places higher demands on transportation systems. It segregates people by income levels, offering each group a different quality of experience living in or near a city. Even young adults—who are rejecting sprawl and car-culture and preferring to live in dense, accessible, and entertaining urban environments such as Charlotte, Austin, Denver, or Seattle—can't really afford to do so.

In the U.S. the growing income gap—and the spatial segregation it promotes—is most extreme in the country's more prosperous and largest cities such as Atlanta, San Francisco, Los Angeles, Chicago, Washington, D.C., and New York. Richard Florida, urban theorist and author, writes "It is not just that the economic divide in America has grown wider; it's that the rich and poor effectively occupy different worlds, even when they live in the same [metropolitan area]." Some refer to this as zip-code inequality.

The "different world" of lower-income neighborhoods that Florida mentions have fewer greenspaces, places to buy healthy food, recreational options, parks, and services such as health clinics and libraries. They often lack easy connections into the transportation network. This lack of access and amenities excludes, marginalizes, and translates into poor health for this group of citizens. Research clearly demonstrates that lower socioeconomic neighborhoods experience higher rates of violent crime, drug use, heart disease, teen pregnancy, and mental illness. Jonathan Rose, in *The Well-Tempered City* argues that when a city only caters to a well-off socioeconomic demographic, over time it will decline. It is not a sustainable city.

We know that to enrich a city through inclusivity and diversity is a positive goal, but it is not enough. Cities must focus on equity. Charles Montgomery, author of *Happy City: Transforming our Lives Through Urban Design,* suggests that cities adopt what he calls an Urban Equity Doctrine. This isn't an actual document or piece of legislation. It is the idea that cities must respect all its citizens before it can expect *all* its citizens to respect, and contribute to, the city in return. It's the idea that, while it is not realistic to have equality in incomes, cities can strive for equality in other measures of quality of life. We know from research into happiness and well-being that residents of varying income levels can be equally happy. How? By sharing the wealth of a city. By giving everyone access and opportunity to enjoy the best assets a city has to offer in terms of public spaces, services, and amenities without feeling unwelcome or inferior. More broadly the Urban Equity Doctrine represents a way of thinking about cities as ecological systems where the health of the entire system is necessary for the well-being of all residents, even the wealthy.

Policy strategies to achieve an equitable city vary greatly around the world. For example, to target the problem of affordable housing in Bristol, England, city officials engage in "neighborhood pepper potting" where they aim for 30% affordable housing (which they define as 25% below market). The good idea here is that the *neighborhood* becomes mixed income, not just the housing. All residents, regardless of income level, have access to the neighborhood amenities they need, feeling comfortable and valued where they live. Bristol's hope is that residents can upgrade their housing without leaving, thus promoting more sustainable and stable neighborhoods.

In its master planning, Singapore divides that mega-city into six sections where each will develop its own downtown core and connect to efficient transit. In another approach, Portland, Oregon's master plan identifies urban hubs of various sizes within the Portland metro area. Hubs are literally circles drawn on the city map around areas that have organically grown in population, typically lower cost areas with access to mass transit. The city then works to develop these hubs into vibrant mixed-use neighborhoods by offering incentives for services and amenities, such as schools, libraries, grocery stores, and health clinics, to cluster within them.

Of course, these efforts require a balancing act. Improvements to lower income neighborhoods—whether bike and pedestrian paths, green space, libraries, better transportation links, or new housing—if not well thought out can create higher land prices and push renters and long-time homeowners out. Top down gentrification of city neighborhoods has become a significant polarizing issue.

Whatever the policy approach, to be inviting, cities must care for *all* its citizens. "It is misguided to try and resurrect a city through 'big project' public policy," writes Edward Glaeser, author of *The Triumph of the City*. "Shiny new real estate may dress up a declining city, but it doesn't solve its underlying problems … Cities are people."

3/

Inspiring People

Scholars and observers of people's behavior within urban environments understand that public spaces communicate using a *silent language.* Ideally, the design of public spaces, along with the activities that occur in them, send messages that invite, inspire, and connect people in ways that enhance civic identity and pride.

This chapter focuses on the important role of creative messaging as part of a city's silent language. Quite simply, the best cities communicate a creative vibe. They engender a sense of enjoyment or inspiration for everyone. Cities might accomplish this, in part, by having a vibrant music or arts scene that populates a city with outdoor concerts, arts festivals, or theater performances in the park. They can foster a business environment that promotes innovation. A city can also send more subtle messages that enhance the experience of walking down the street (3-1).

Understanding the Power of Creative Catalysts

Have you ever laughed at some odd, yet surprising scene you observe (Is that dog really on a skateboard?). Or have you ever used your lunch break to visit a new pocket park or stop to look at an impromptu display of side-walk art? If you have, cognitive scientists would predict that you felt a little more energized later in the day.

Why? What do those experiences have in common? However brief, such moments encourage us to think in different ways using different parts

of our brain. For example, a dog on a skateboard is an unexpected combination of ideas, which according to scientists, activates our imagination. Exploring a new place adds variety to one's day, offering new visual inputs that can promote creative thinking. And research shows that if that place exposes a person to nature, it enhances that possibility even more. And checking out the sidewalk art? Research reveals that experiencing others' creative expression—whether art, poetry, or music—inspires our own creative thinking abilities.

It turns out that researchers know a lot about the conditions that promote creative thinking in individuals or groups: the conditions that inspire individuals to write, play music, paint, or innovate. We call these *creative catalysts*. Creative catalysts are visual prompts or environmental conditions that fire up the parts of our brain known for creative (versus more analytical) thought processes. Understanding creative catalysts offers valuable insights for making better cities because when the parts of the brain more associated with creative thinking activate, people tend to feel more energized, relaxed, and even happier. And if those creative catalysts appear in our cityscape, well, then people will tend to feel more energized, relaxed, and even happier when in public spaces.

Looked at another way, understanding creative catalysts helps to explain *why* people prefer certain spaces and activities in a city. Taking stock of his midtown Manhattan surroundings, one *New York Times* journalist observed that creativity attracts people. He wrote, "A beer garden made out of freight containers on an empty plot turns out to be a lot more popular and better for a city than a sad corporate atrium with a few café tables and a long list of don'ts on the wall."

What follows are some proven types of creative catalysts easily given form in urban environments through a city's design, programs, and policies. These include the catalysts of unexpected associations, variety, nature, humor, art, and elements of play.

Encourage the Unexpected

One very effective catalyst for creative thinking is to ask a person to experience, or try to connect, two disparate concepts as one. Writers employ this strategy often when they use literary techniques such as metaphor or juxtaposition to delight and engage their readers. Businesses use this technique to brainstorm new ideas for products or services. People enjoy the cognitive jolt of experiencing something unexpected in a mundane situation. We use the term *unexpected associations* to describe this creative catalyst. Bringing together disparate ideas, here and there, in urban settings, can add a bit of delight and inspiration.

Functional Art

By necessity cities are full of the functional and the mundane. Garbage cans, utility boxes, manholes, downspouts. Why must these be ugly? One way to create unexpected associations in a city is to jazz up these bland urban essentials into *functional art.*

Many cities have discovered that trash and recycling bins can be a venue for exhibiting art, such as these colorful receptacles in Charlotte, North Carolina (3-2). In Curitiba, Brazil recycling bins shaped like bongos make the mundane more attractive, as well as offer a proud salute to Brazilian culture (3-3).

What could be duller than a drainpipe? This downspout on a building in Madrid, with its wide-open fish mouth, provides a bit of subtle artistry while doing its job directing water running off the roof (3-4). Not nearly as subtle, but even more fun is a drain pipe painted like a cactus in Vitoria-Gasteiz in Basque, Spain (3-5).

3-2

3-3

3-4

3-5

3-6   3-7

In Nanaimo and Victoria, British Columbia most of the electrical and traffic control boxes display unique artwork or photographs depicting nature and historical scenes. Other cities, from Dublin, Ireland (3-6) to Auckland, New Zealand (3-7) support their own expressions of this genre of functional art. Such efforts not only brighten the streetscape but can support local artists and deter graffiti. Cities have discovered that graffiti artists prefer blank canvases and rarely tag over another artists' work. There are different approaches a city might take to sprucing up utility boxes. In Auckland, the city hired a single artist to paint many utility boxes. In Boston, the Boston Art Commission's Paintbox Program solicits applications from local area artists. To apply, one must live and work in the city limits. Artists receive a stipend, and no single artist can paint more than three utility boxes. In Fremont, California city officials hope to paint 160 utility boxes through its box*ART!* program. The box*ART!* program asks local artists to propose designs that express themes of sustainability, green energy, innovation, technology, community, ecology, education, or the arts. It then pairs each selected artist with a business, organization, or individual sponsor to support the cost.

It's hard to imagine manhole covers as the subject for books, photo exhibitions, and travel and art media coverage around the world. But in Japan, manhole covers are magnificent, such as this one from Hakodate (3-8). The backstory is that in the mid 1980s a high-ranking official in the country's construction ministry came up with the idea for municipalities to customize their manhole covers. The idea took off, and the competition began as each municipality tried to design the most unique manhole cover. An estimated 6,000 artistic manholes later (and even a Japan Society of Manhole Covers), these tiny art treasures are a source of local pride throughout the country.

Street furniture and bike racks lend themselves to artistic expression as well. Melbourne creates "sit-able" art by adding some very ornate sidewalk benches (3-9). Rzeszów, Poland adds some color to the streets with bike racks (3-10).

Subway stations, bus stops, and public restrooms can also offer canvases for community expression beyond advertising. In the Highlandtown neighborhood of Baltimore this typographic bus stop not only acts as a conversation piece, but protects bus stop visitors from heat and rain while offering a place to sit. It has also become a meeting point within the community (3-11).

Perhaps these examples from West Bromwich, England (3-12) and Kawakawa, New Zealand take public toilet architecture to the extreme, but they do make the point that a public restroom need not be ugly. The colorful public toilet in Kawakawa, designed by famed Austrian artist Friedensreich Hundertwasser, is a tourist attraction—inside and out—for this North Island town (3-13).

3-8

3-9

3-10

3-11

3-12

3-13

3-16

Uncommon Spaces

Another type of unexpected association is to place a function, activity, or behavior in an unusual location. This creative combination offers a sense of delight for those using these spaces in a different way. The Ponyfish Island bar and restaurant, located on a floating pylon under the pedestrian bridge that crosses the Yarra River in Melbourne, is a popular and unusual spot that provides a unique perspective of the city day and night (3-14).

Sandy beach, lounge chairs, and palm trees in the middle of Berlin or Paris? Why not? Paris Plages is a popular summer happening, conceived in 2002 by Paris Mayor Bertrand Delanoë, that creates a series of artificial beaches along the River Seine during July and August (3-15). Visitors lounge on beach chairs, enjoy free evening concerts, kayak, and socialize. Like Paris, Berlin is nowhere near an ocean, but the city trucks in artificial sand to create beach settings at various spots along the River Spree, complete with beach bars, restaurant, and beach volleyball.

Or, why not go surfing on that urban river? In 1972, the city inserted some concrete blocks to break up the current on Munich's Eisbach River

3-14 3-15 3-17

creating a permanent wave. For years surfers illegally got their thrills. In 2010 surfing on the Eisbach became legal, drawing throngs of surfers, and even more spectators (3-16). Munich isn't the only landlocked city with a surf scene. Cities in Switzerland, Norway, and China also offer this urban sport.

Power Plant Svartsengi, the first geothermal combined heat and power plant of its kind, sits near Reykjavik, Iceland in a stark, moon-like lava landscape. Located between two continents, the Euro-Asian and American tectonic plates meet under this location, creating an active volcano system. This allows for super-hot, mineral- and algae-rich water to vent up from the ground to run turbines that generate electricity. The water and steam that leave the turbines then pass through a heat exchanger, providing heat for a municipal water system. The hot water discharge flows into a lake that holds almost 1.6 million gallons, refreshed every 40 hours. Instead of banning people from the area, a typical utility practice, the power company decided to develop recreational and medicinal uses for the surplus water. This uncommon space is now a world-class spa known as the Blue Lagoon. The site attracts around 400,000 annual visitors, making it Iceland's top tourist attraction (3-17).

The expectation is to go to an opera house in fancy dress for an evening of high-brow culture. Or, we could go to play! In Oslo, city planners built an opera house that is also, and contrary to expectations, a public park. Completed in 2008, the building includes a public access rooftop that angles down to a large iceberg-shaped granite public plaza ending at the water's edge (3-18). Designed to inspire, not to intimidate (even skateboarders are welcome), this juxtaposition of public space use attracts locals and visitors – in evening gowns and bathing suits alike.

3-18

3-19

The Rooftop Cinema in the heart of the central business district of Melbourne, Australia provides open air viewing all summer long of cult classic, art house, and recently released films. Located on top of a seven-story 1922 Art Nouveau building, moviegoers can kick back on the 160 deck chairs with a glass of wine and something to eat while watching stars on the screen and in the sky (3-19). The well-lit skyscrapers that surround the cinema enhance the evening ambiance. On cool nights, moviegoers can rent blankets, the proceeds of which go to the Melbourne City Mission and homeless shelter. This theater-on-a-rooftop concept is not unique to Melbourne. Owner Barry Barton got the idea from a visit to New York,

3-20

44

3-21

3-22

where he came across a portable movie theater that moved to different buildings throughout the summer. Other cities, such as Perth, Australia and Los Angeles, have embraced this uncommon use of space by putting theaters on top of parking garages.

The new Amager Bakke waste-to-energy plant in Copenhagen provides 97% of city homes with heating and about 4,000 people with electricity. So what makes it an uncommon space? This innovative project by BIG-Bjarke Ingels Group incorporates a functional ski run, hiking trails, and climbing wall into the rooftop design as shown in this rendering (3-20). Unlike other energy-intensive artificial ski slopes, this one uses a recycled synthetic granular material. Planters wrap the building, now the highest spot in Copenhagen, creating a green facade that looks like a mountain from a distance.

Check messages while waiting for your train? That's so yesterday. Why not tend to your tomatoes? Yes, why not put a farm on a train station? The East Japan Railway Company located five "Soradofarms" on its rail network. The first was at Tokyo's Ebisu station (3-21). People can rent a plot and tend their vegetables prior to catching the train. No need to bring your bucket, the train station supplies essential equipment, seeds, and even advice for commuters new to the relaxing pastime of gardening. These rooftop gardens on train stations have proven very popular with wait lists to get a plot.

Artists, of course, thrive on creating uncommon associations. This London bus stop, designed by Bruno Taylor, combines a mundane space and function (waiting for a bus) with a touch of fun by installing a swing, resulting in a delightful and uncommon experience (3-22).

Plan for Variety

Do you eat the same thing for breakfast each day? Go the same way to work? Get your news from the same source? While humans often feel safe in their daily routines, research overwhelmingly points to the importance of variety as a catalyst for creativity. Conversely, a lack of variety dulls our senses and diminishes an awareness of our surroundings. Applying this knowledge to cities, we all know what happens when variety is lacking. We've seen this in the failures of suburban tract housing or rows of tenement housing in city planning. If one's environment is too dull, repetitious or static, it loses its appeal – and our pride in it. In his book *Happy City*, Charles Montgomery offers examples of how efforts to simplify cities through rational design and order most often fail. Using the example of Brasilia, he found that people preferred their cramped market streets and the complex disorder of typical Brazilian cities. So, for a city to inspire people, it must abound in variety.

Variation in Setting

City Layout. First, one can express variety in city layout. Dover and Massengale, in their book *Street Design: The Secret to Great Cities and Towns*, advocate against a dominance of grids and classifications and for variation in a city's overall street design and layout. Some grids make sense, but overall cities should contain streets of varying widths, ranging from alley to street to boulevard. Cities should have streets designated for different speeds and purposes – some that are fast and car friendly, others that are slow and bike friendly, and yet others that meander with interesting elements for pedestrians to enjoy.

Neighborhood Variety. The variety of shops, services, and housing that characterize a mixed-use neighborhood offers multiple benefits for cities and its residents. Mixed-use areas encourage walking, reduce traffic and pollution, and increase a sense of community and social interaction. In the U.S., studies show that mixed-use neighborhoods have lower crime rates. Kensington Market is a diverse Toronto neighborhood. It boasts a mash-up of wide and narrow streets, Rastafari stores, a farmers' market, bars, restaurants, a synagogue, clothing stores, and a vibrant music scene. On a Sunday in Bellevue Square Park, shown here, people might be dancing, kicking soccer balls,

3-23   3-24   3-27

3-25   3-26

using a hula hoop, or playing musical instruments. Such variation within a relatively small area makes the neighborhood come alive (3-23).

Street-level variety. Jan Gehl's concept of soft edges is, by definition, visual variety. Soft edges are streetscapes that are varied, dynamic, textured, and detailed at eye level. The architecture might combine old and new. The buildings and sidewalk features might combine materials that are rough and smooth. The street facade might offer visual treats of color or nature as shown in the side street in Elburg, Netherlands (3-24).

Flexible and Temporary Use of Spaces

Cities can build more variation into the urban experience by supporting the flexible and temporary use of public spaces. Public places that can shift in look or activity depending on the time of day, day of the week, month, or season offer more possibilities for more people of all ages to enjoy their city surroundings.

Campo de' Fiori, located in the heart of Rome, begins each day as a bustling one-stop shopping market for fruits, vegetables, meats, spices, flowers, and kitchen supplies (3-25). By evening the stands are down, the

3-28   3-29   3-30

area cleaned, and the Campo de' Fiori transforms into another type of social gathering space with families, friends, and couples strolling, dining, and listening the music that pervades the evening space (3-26). At other times it might host protests or festivals.

Paris is one of the premier cities in the world for its variety and number of outdoor and indoor public markets, featuring art, antiques, books, collectibles, fashion, food, and drink. On Thursdays, Saturdays, and Sundays regulars and tourists visit the Marché aux Timbres on the Champs Elysées for stamps or postcards. Once a month Le Marché Rétro d'Oberkampf offers unique finds of vintage fashion and furniture. Every weekend, Marché aux Puces de St-Oeun, perhaps the biggest flea market in the world, draws regulars and tourists alike (3-27). Some markets are weekends, once a week, once a month, every two months, or a few times a year like the popular pop-up store at Hôtel Bohême. The way Paris markets blend variety, with regularity, is an ideal formula.

Another way for cities to embrace variation through flexible use is by opening streets to allow for unique activities or events to occur. In Mexico City, there are nearly 40 miles of bike lanes. Plus, every Sunday morning Avenida Reforma, typically grid-locked with traffic during the week, becomes a wildly popular pedestrian, roller skating, stroller, and bicycling party, drawing 10,000 or more participants each week and spawning water tents, free bike repair, food carts, and outdoor exercise classes along the way (3-28). And that's not all. Once a month a 20-mile circuit of traffic-free streets open. This Cicloton event can attract close to 70,000 cyclists. Cities around the world are doing the same, annually, seasonally, monthly, or even weekly. The goal is to promote activities that benefit the environment and people's health, but the effect is to "change it up" and foster community spirit through variety. It's fun and empowering to take over the streets.

Bristol is a city in Southwest England that embraces all things livable and sustainable. Once a shipping port, then heavily bombarded in WWII, this mid-size city reinvented itself into a great place to live, a top tourist destination, and recipient of Europe's Green City award. Much progress occurred under the leadership of former mayor George Ferguson. One of mayor Ferguson's greatest areas of impact was to make Bristol a city for families and kids. Today, the city boasts safe spaces to play, bike, walk, and participate in lots of family-oriented events and programs. For example, he introduced the "Make Sunday Special" program which allows neighborhoods to propose activities they would like to host on their street. Unlike a neighborhood block party, the city-sanctioned Sunday events are open to everyone in town. On any given Make Sunday Special day, three or more streets might participate. The first year of this program saw a giant water slide (3-29) (crowdfunded by the community), music performances, dance workshops, craft classes for kids, balloon modeling, ping pong tables in the street, sofas to lounge on, giant chess boards, improv theater, book readings, magicians, hula-hoop workshops, and more. A terrific success, Make Sunday Special is a dynamic use of city space that builds community and makes Bristol a fun and inspiring place to live.

The VIVA Vancouver program, sponsored through the Engineering Department in Vancouver, British Columbia, also encourages creative input from the community to temporarily transform streets into fun friendly spaces. Community groups propose the location, frequency, and theme. VIVA Vancouver tests, monitors, and evaluates the events. If successful, the event might become a regular activity. For example, after its initial trial run, Granville Street now regularly closes on weekends throughout the summer for a variety of art, music, dance, or food festivals (3-30). Contrary to conventional wisdom, local businesses love these temporary and varied events as they draw many more people into each area.

Some city spaces vary season to season. Within the large Millennium Park complex in Chicago, the McCormick Tribune Plaza is Chicago's largest outdoor dining complex. Much of the year it hosts music and culinary events (3-31). Then from mid-November to mid-March it becomes a free, public ice-skating rink attracting over 100,000 skaters annually (3-32).

3-31

3-32

3-33

3-34

3-35

Every city has spaces that are in transition: vacant lots, empty storefronts, or construction sites. Whether vacant for months or years, these sites can attract criminal activity or just become unsightly. A 2014 report by the U.S. Department of Housing and Urban Development (HUD) promotes the idea of "Temporary Urbanism" by encouraging cities to have policies, regulations, and programs that support the temporary use of city or privately-owned lots or spaces. Many cities are now making positive, short-term use of transitional spaces. This is a terrific way to add variation to a city.

Empty storefronts tell the wrong story in a city. They speak of tough times, instability, or a lack of vibrancy within a neighborhood. Left too long, they communicate a lack of safety as the blank canvas attracts vandalism.

Inspiring People

3-36

Joan Vorderbruggen of Hennepin Theatre Trust in Minneapolis looks at empty storefronts and sees the perfect stage to showcase the works of local artists, all the while keeping every city block alive. Vorderbruggen launched the extremely successful "Made Here" program. The Made Here program features artists' works (such as this one by Quinn Rivenburgh) temporarily installed in vacant storefronts within an area of 15 city blocks (3-33), creating an outdoor urban art gallery and inspiring walking tour. The semiannual exhibition lasts for four months. Vorderbruggen's commitment to a vibrant and diverse downtown district emphasizes Made Here artists from communities of color. She hopes that programs such as Made Here will encourage property owners to see creative, temporary installations in vacant spaces as a boon to business by attracting future tenants to see the potential energy of an area.

Integrate Art, Humor, and Nature

It should come as no surprise that art, humor, and nature are creative catalysts. And sometimes, it doesn't take much. Simple, stationary metal balls in public spaces in Barcelona bring out the playfulness in children and adults alike (3-34, 3-35). The Zinneke (Flemish for mongrel) found along Rue des Chartreux in Brussels always brings a smile to unsuspecting visitors to the neighborhood (3-36). Artist Tom Frantzen created this street sculpture in 1999 to express a form of humor that allow passersby to share in a little absurd fun.

3-37   3-38

We've all watched our sandcastles wash away with the rising tide at the beach. If we were a little kid, we might have even shed a tear. Ann Arbor, Michigan artist David Zinn watches the rain wash away his outdoor chalk art all the time and claims, "it doesn't bother me a bit." First, his chalk art isn't his livelihood. It's his contribution to city living. Zinn believes that "more art in more places ... make people more cheerful." Zinn's chalk art, however, embodies some characteristics that speak to the essence of play and inspiration. First, his drawings are anamorphic (3D-like, also known as *trompe l'oeil*) (3-37). They appear to pop out of the pavement when one walks by. This is art that reaches out and grabs people. His art is also humorous (think green blob monsters, flying pigs, and lots of mice), playing off features of the natural or built environment. A tuft of grass might become a character's hair or another character might crawl out of a sidewalk crack. Although Zinn drawings appear in other cities as part of art festivals or city-sanctioned invitations, in Ann Arbor his guerilla chalk art is perfectly legal (in many cities it would not be). Because these entertaining characters appear on public property and are not permanent, city officials have decided that Zinn creations, and other chalk art like them, can be fun for everyone – at least until it rains.

3-39

Glasgow finally decided to embrace its long, and at times contentious, history with street artists and taggers to create the City Centre Mural Trail. Launched in 2008, this initiative showcased talented, local artists by supporting large-scale murals (both temporary and permanent) on buildings, fences, and overpass walls. The murals vary in subject matter from animals, to sports, to edgy humor. Visitors can easily walk to see the 14 murals using a map provided by the city. The idea of the mural trail was to enlist local street artists to revitalize and promote the city center. One humorous mural on the trail is "Honey I Shrunk the Kids" by Australian-born, but Glasgow-based Smug (aka Sam Bates) located on Mitchell Street (3-38). The woman seems to be picking up cars (or people) depending where one stands.

Exposure to nature is a well-proven creative catalyst. But sometimes bringing more greenery into dense city layouts requires as much creativity as it may inspire. The High Line project in New York City is an elevated linear park project that benefits multiple neighborhoods of a city (3-39). This Lower West Side public park sits on the remnants of an elevated rail line that hovered above rail yards and warehouses of the former meat-packing district. It was the hardy plants that self-seeded and grew along the original freight rail bed and during its 25-years of abandonment that inspired the landscape design. The result is 1.45 miles of bio-diverse, sustainable, native species offering different patterns of texture and color

3-40

to visitors each season. Innovative projects such as the elevated High Line demonstrate that parks do not have to be flat areas of grass taking up a city block. They can also reclaim and repurpose abandoned industrial sites, connecting a park to a city's history. Linear parks spur adjacent development across many neighborhoods, not just in one. Friends of the High Line, a non-profit conservancy, maintains the park, which is owned by the City of New York.

Sometimes inspiration from nature appears in the smallest of spaces. Guerrilla gardening is an international movement to connect people to nature one plant, one nook, and one cranny at a time. Advocates of guerrilla gardening beautify decrepit medians, abandoned lots, or the ugly base around streetlight poles, usually without city permission. It's hardly a new idea for citizens to volunteer to beautify neighborhood spaces, but the guerrilla gardening movement also brings with it a message of protest about the lack of nature and beauty in cities. They often target neglected public or private property. These activist gardeners are surprisingly widespread (in close to 40 countries) and organized, employing forums, websites, books, how-to video, workshops, and TED talks to share successes and strategies. They exchange tips on topics such as planting community vegetable gardens, distributing "seed bombs," container gardening in abandoned tires, or painting with moss graffiti. In Brussels one guerrilla gardening group plants sunflowers throughout the city (3-40).

Remember to Play

A range of urban movements exist hoping to improve cities. We hear about smart cities, green cities, slow cities, and more. One of these is the playable cities movement. Advocates for this movement want play woven into the

3-41   3-42

urban experience because it engages people with the city. Play also attracts people, especially families, to public spaces making them vibrant and safe. Play is healthy psychologically, physically, and socially. Cognitive scientists also identify play as a prompt to creative thinking. So, promoting *elements of play* in urban environments is another type of creative catalyst.

In playful cities, officials support spaces like all-ages playgrounds. They provide street permits for fun events on city boulevards or for neighborhood play streets for kids. They put musical instruments in parks. They support "sort of crazy" events like Seattle's Green Lake Milk Carton derby where people race home-built milk carton boats, or the naked Solstice bike parade in the nearby Fremont neighborhood.

Who doesn't love a little "whoopdeedoo" in their day? To promote Bike to Work Week in Vancouver, B.C., Canadian designer Greg Papove and graphic artist Claire Balderston installed a series of Whoopdeedoo ramps on a selection of bike lanes to promote a bit of fun for the city's bicycle commuters (3-41).

Yarn bombs offer another expression of fun and, at times protest (AKA guerilla knitting, fiber art, yarnstorming, graffiti knitting, or grandma graffiti). Media attention to this practice dates to 2002 when artist Shannon Schollian knit "stump cozies" to protest the clear cutting of trees in Oregon. Soon artists in other parts of the U.S. yarn bombed chain-link fences, stop signs, benches, utility boxes, and broken pay phones to add a bit of color and whimsy, especially to areas of urban blight. Since then the practice has grown in popularity in Canada and across Europe, spawning books, documentaries, International Yarnbombing Day (Canada), and plenty of

3-43

3-44

tourist photographs. This photo is a yarn bombing in Madrid (3-42). While technically illegal, cities consider yarn bombs relatively harmless as they don't damage a surface or structure like spray paint. A pair of scissors easily removes the yarn. (Although if left too long in inclement weather, the yarn degrades and can end up in stormwater drains.) These playful activists knit or crochet panels in advance, then tie them together to wrap around objects. This might happen in the middle of the night for an element of surprise or in daylight to invite interaction with passersby. To add to the sense of play, yarn bombers often have pun-filled, superhero style names. The original members of the Knit the City group in London are Deadly Knitshade, Knitting Ninja, Lady Loop, Bluestocking Stitching, and the Purple Purl.

The mission of the Red Swing Project is simple: "We strive to positively impact under-utilized public spaces with simple red swings." Fun! Here, a boy in Austin, Texas, where the Red Swing project launched in 2007, helps to assemble a $2 swing made from painted wood and retired rock-climbing rope (3-43). The idea came from a group of architecture students who promoted the idea online by providing instructions and a how-to video for setting up your own swing. It caught on. People are swinging on the project's red swings in the United States, India, Thailand, Brazil, Taiwan, South Korea, France, Spain, Portugal, Haiti, Poland, Italy, Germany, and Australia. Besides bringing a smile or nostalgic moment from childhood as one takes a ride, each red swing has a unique number so users can share their experiences online. As one person posted: "I found swing #035 below the L in Bucktown, Chicago, IL. The swing/this project has made my day! I spent a good 20 minutes swinging. I laughed out loud each time the train passed over me. A toddler looked at me with envy from her stroller. A

Inspiring People

3-45

worker offered to give me a big push. My happiness seemed to rub off on people passing by."

Speaking of swings, the public interactive project, 21 Balançoires (21 Swings) is a series of large swing sets installed in Quartier des Spectacles in Montreal, Canada that, together, create a giant collective musical instrument (3-44). Each swing, when in motion, produces notes from a different type of instrument (e.g., guitar, piano, harp). The higher the person swings, the higher the note. When people cooperate, swinging simultaneously or at coordinated intervals and at different heights, they create a unique musical composition. At night, the swings light up, adding even more magic to the experience. Launched in 2011, the 21 Swings project creators Mouna Andraos and Melissa Mongiat of Daily Tour les Jours said it was the idea of community cooperation through fun that inspired them. They wanted to create a public place for people of all ages and backgrounds to play and hang out, while at the same time, sending a message about the benefits of diverse groups working together to achieve more than an individual can accomplish alone. The popular 21 Balançoires appear every spring.

3-46

3-47

Inspiring People

Who doesn't love a fountain? Decorative fountains ask for visual appreciation, but interactive fountains beg for people to play. And frankly, any experience that allows kids to squeal and get wet (from fire hydrant to fountain) is going to be a success. This is the philosophy of Danish artist Jeppe Hein who created, among others, the "Appearing Rooms" fountain at Forrest Place in Perth, Australia. Installed in 2012, the fountain was part of a larger redevelopment plan intended to give more functional and artistic life to a historic, but staid area in the city's center. The water feature is a grid of nine "rooms" where walls of water rise and fall around each room, randomly, every 10 seconds (3-45). This creates a game element where people can get "caught" in or outside of a water room. The interactive element was crucial to the project. Heins said, "I see my artwork as a tool for communication and dialogue ... people are drawn to the water and begin to experience other people." Of course, playable fountains must take care to protect the health of people, as well as not squander water. To supply the fountain, the City of Perth collects, recycles, and chlorinates stormwater to be swimming pool quality.

The popular Crown Fountain in Chicago's Millennium Park is part public art, part fountain, and part video experience (3-46). Completed in 2004 (designed by Catalan artist Jaume Plensa), the fountain consists of a granite reflecting pool between two 50-foot, glass brick towers. Light-emitting diodes behind the transparent bricks display digital videos of a diverse cross-section of 1,000 Chicago residents' faces. Every five minutes or so, the water streaming down the towers spouts out of a nozzle at the center of the face's puckered lips—like a digital gargoyle—to everyone's delight. The images are on display year-round, while the water fountain operates mid-spring to mid-autumn. Crown Fountain, while a controversial and expensive venture at $17 million, now is a beloved part of the city's culture, offering a popular public gathering space, free interactive entertainment, and an escape from heat (3-47).

Urban games are another type of play that cities can support. Here, the cityscape becomes a game board. The contests might be high or low tech, but most involve interactivity, cooperation, and navigation within a city. They might be video-game or board game inspired. They can be educational or just entertainment. They might be mostly competitive or collaborative. They can be free or paid. In fact, urban gaming is spreading around the globe, from human-scale Pac-Man games in New York ("Pac-Manhatten") to nighttime zombie hunts across the United Kingdom to Pokémon Go and geocaching in cities around the world. Some cities opt to promote more educational games where participants learn about the local history, architecture, or art of a city. For example, two creative professionals from Copenhagen designed an urban treasure hunt where participants search for a series of clues at temporary artworks or installations placed around the city. At each station, searchers find an orange dot with a number inside (3-48). Participants collect these numbers and use them to open a treasure chest at the end. The Copenhagen duo then paired with some artists to stage a similar treasure hunt in Budapest, with a route that highlights that city's Art Nouveau buildings. As one organizer stated, the goal is to "experience the city in a totally new way. You start to look at your surroundings in a different light and begin to notice things you had never seen before."

Creative catalysts woven into a cityscape activate the parts of people's brains associated with creative thought and imagination. This, in turn, contributes to a person's sense of engagement and well-being as they experience public spaces. The examples in this chapter underscore several themes that run throughout this book. First, small ideas can make a difference, whether a brightly colored utility box or a swing at a bus stop. Second, cities need to be open to dynamic and diverse uses for public spaces. Why not open a street for a tango dancing night? Third, local artists are natural partners in making cities feel vibrant and fun. Many of the examples throughout this chapter of functional art, uncommon spaces, nature, humor, and play involve artists in key roles. Finally, cities are places to live and work, but also to play. People increasingly choose to live in cities based on lifestyle and quality of life factors such as culture, entertainment, health, and the arts. Using our knowledge of creative catalysts, cities of any size can feel lively and dynamic.

3-48

61

4/

Connecting People

A sustainable city is one that improves the quality of human life while living within the carrying capacity of supporting ecosystems. We like this definition because it suggests sustainability is more than preserving our environment for future generations; it's also about improving people's lives. It reflects the "three pillars" view of sustainability, emphasizing the need for cities to pursue environmental, economic, and social sustainability.

This chapter focuses on social sustainability: the capacity of current and future generations to create and maintain strong communities. Communities that are cohesive, equitable, cooperative, healthy and resilient. Communities where diverse people have the ability and commitment to work together toward common goals. To achieve this requires connecting people to each other and to the place where they live.

Unfortunately, just as cities face environmental and economic challenges, they also grapple with social challenges. While the exact figures vary depending on the source, in the United States the percent of citizens who report feeling socially isolated has increased from 10% in the mid-1980s to 25% of all citizens today. Twenty-five percent! And, researchers find that feelings of social isolation intensify in communities that experience racial, cultural, or ethnic divides, marginalization, discrimination, or threat. This weakening of social cohesion is a trend that cities simply must work to reverse, as without social sustainability we have little chance of achieving environmental and economic sustainability.

So, this tour continues by exploring good ideas for connecting people in positive ways.

Build Communication-Rich Environments

Achieving social sustainability requires the building of *social capital*: networks of people who are willing to do things for each other – and by extension for their city. Social capital is best thought of as the social and psychological well-being and sense of belonging people feel when part of a community. It's the glue that holds communities together. The key ingredients of social capital are norms of trust, reciprocity, collaboration, and information exchange. When these are present, and strong, people are willing to do things for each other; they are willing to pursue common goals.

Every city has formal institutions such as schools, churches, or work-places that contribute to the building of social capital. Ray Oldenburg, author of the seminal book *The Great Good Place*, coined the term "third place" to refer to the informal spaces that also foster social interaction and a sense of community life. He mentions coffee shops, restaurants, parks, libraries, community centers, bars, hair salons, clubs, markets, or book-stores. According to Oldenburg, these private and public places function as third places if they are accessible and welcoming, and when conversation is the main activity.

While we like the concept of a third place, we promote a type of "enhanced" third place called a *Communication-Rich Environment (CRE)*. A communication-rich environment is more than the local café or bar hosting the same familiar faces (and conversations) each day. These are indeed important, but have limits, particularly as more people seem to prefer screens to conversations. Communication-rich environments promote social connection, but in ways more relevant to today's cities. Cities that are faster-paced, more diverse, and more dynamic in the ways people interact.

One important distinction from Oldenburg's third place concept is that CREs foster *lite relationships*. These are relationships that develop to a degree where people are willing to trust, reciprocate, collaborate, and

4-1   4-3

exchange information, but are short of the pressures and constraints that can accompany familial or close friend relationships. In our personal lives we, of course, value depth of attachment and intimacy. For public life, the building of social sustainability is about the development of large and fluid networks of lite relationships.

Another important distinction is that CREs invite *diversity* in types of people and in the types of communication that occur. Diverse members of a community should feel equally comfortable and safe engaging in multiple and rich forms of discourse. They can: listen and observe; get advice and helpful information; share news, information, and stories; and freely express and exchange opinions. They can also come together to: collaborate; present or perform; celebrate, mourn, and reflect; learn; solve problems; and envision new ideas.

And, unlike Oldenburg's third place, CREs can be places, spaces, or events, permanent or temporary, physical or online, as long as they are tied to a particular neighborhood or geographic community.

The traditional symbol of a CRE is the central public square, a site for celebration, protest, mourning, meeting, performances, speeches, and exchange. Whether the Piazza del Campo in Siena, Italy, the Old Town Square in Prague, Czech Republic (4-1), or Plaza de la Constitución in Oaxaca, Mexico these spaces have never lost their role in the social and political life of their city.

Sadly, in some older cities these traditional squares have died out or

4-2

succumbed to market forces to become only a place to shop. In many newer cities or their suburbs, they never existed. That is starting to change. Melbourne created Federation Square as part of a plan to bring life back to the city center. Opening in 2002, Federation Square is an eclectic collection of buildings that includes the Australian Center for Moving Images, galleries, restaurants, and bars (4-2). Despite some critiques of the bold architecture, this large public space is communication rich in that diverse people and types of communication appear there. Thousands of people a year gather to watch sports events on the big screen, participate in hip hop contests, protest, celebrate, mourn, or just enjoy the amenities. It has become an important communicative space for seminal events. Here former Australian Prime Minister Kevin Rudd delivers his 2008 national apology to the Stolen Generations of Australia, children of Australian Aboriginal and Torres Strait Islander descent taken from their homes as part of government policy for close to 50 years (4-3).

4-4

4-5

How do cities foster social connectivity beyond the central square? To answer that, one needs to identify the conditions that promote communication-rich environments.

Informal and Relaxed

To begin, CREs express a sense of informality and conviviality that enhances conversation. So, while political rallies and town meetings play important roles in the communicative space of a city, it's not at those events where social capital is built. It is in the unscripted spaces and at informal events where the most diverse and productive community interactions occur.

In the U.S. the block party is a great example of the benefits of informal spaces and events. Block parties can happen anytime (although typically in the summer), but most occur on the first Tuesday in August each year. In 1984 the National Association of Town Watch (NATW) promoted the first National Night Out (NNO) across the United States. The origin of the event was, and still is, based on the belief that cohesive, healthy neighborhoods are keys to preventing crime and violence. In fact, police, firefighters, and park rangers often visit block parties to show a friendly face. Over 38 million people across 50 states come together for block parties largely because they are informal and social. Neighbors take over the street, roll out the barbeque, and bring kids, games, and food. Minneapolis ranks #1 in the U.S. for participation in NNO with close to 1,500 events on 2,440 blocks in 2014 (4-4).

4-6   4-7

Comfortable to Converse

CREs allow people to comfortably converse in normal tones, seated or strolling one-on-one or in groups. Traffic noise shouldn't drown out conversations. This might seem obvious, but there are many city spaces where this isn't the case. This small urban park in Santa Monica offers locals a place away from tourists, beachfront glitz, and expensive shops to tell stories and make connections (4-5).

Pedestrian areas like this one in Jerusalem (4-6) serve many purposes including being a place for regular and spontaneous connecting with people. Here again, the absence of traffic noise allows for normal conversations to occur. One revealing study compared three demographically similar neighborhoods in San Francisco. In the neighborhood with the lowest level of car traffic and noise, residents reported three times as many friends and two times as many acquaintances from the neighborhood.

Pull up a seat. Urban planning gurus from William H. Whyte to Jane Jacobs to Jan Gehl have long pointed out the importance of public seating that allows both comfort and choice. Movable chairs, such as in the MoMa sculpture garden in New York City (4-7), allow visitors to socialize, retreat for some quiet time, or move to the sun or shade. Although more cost efficient and comfortable than fixed benches, cities have been reluctant to use movable chairs for fear of theft. However, evidence suggests that this concern is overblown. New York City parks officials report that, yes, they lose a few chairs a year, but overall the benefits greatly outweigh any loss. They also offer some strategies to deter theft: 1) staff the parks (an employee wipes down, stacks, and locks chairs at the end of the day); 2) shift the management role to adjacent businesses, property owners, or neighborhood groups (especially for small parks); or 3) use chairs that are plain and inexpensive, heavy, or branded.

Fluidity

The concept of fluidity is key to the building of vibrant social networks. Applied to public spaces, fluidity means that people come and go, by the hour, day, week, or year so social interactions do not stagnate. Pocket parks are small public spaces created by cities on vacant or irregular lots of land or street rights-of-way. They provide a refuge for people to meet, rest, have lunch, or just read a book. The smaller scale of the space encourages interactions (or a sense of quiet camaraderie). Pocket parks are also fluid. People come and go. In the United States, the appearance of "vest" pocket parks dates to the 1967 Paley's Park and 1971 Greenacre Park, both in New York City. Both of are examples of foundation-funded and award-winning designs that include waterfalls and sophisticated landscaping. Today, pocket parks might be as simple as a picnic table and potted plant on an unused triangle of intersection pavement. Whatever the design, pocket parks should

4-8

Connecting People

4-9

be highly visible to invite people and discourage illegal activity – as this one in Abingdon Square Park, New York City (4-8). Popular pocket parks also have low ambient noise levels to encourage conversation, moveable chairs and tables, trash receptacles that are frequently emptied, and offer some protection from the elements (shade tree, wind block, or a heat lamp).

One size smaller than a pocket park, a parklet is the use of two parking spaces (or similar street space) to create a place for people to rest, take in the street sights, enjoy a snack, and converse. Each parklet is unique. In addition to seating, they often include bike parking, plants, and a touch of artistic whimsy. Parklets might appear for special events, like International Park[ing] Day, seasonally, or as permanent additions to a street. If year round, cities typically require that they be movable for situations like snow removal or emergencies. The parklet idea originated in San Francisco to encourage people to reimagine streets as public space, while encouraging pedestrian activity, supporting local business, beautifying areas, and promoting community. Since then, city parklet programs have spread through the United States and elsewhere. Financial support and designs for parklets come from businesses, community organizations, or residents in cooperation with the city. This parklet is on Noriega Street in San Francisco (4-9).

Conversation Prompts

Researchers, such as ethnographers, who interview people in the field have long known that having a third point of reference, like an object or photo, as a conversation prompt makes it more comfortable for strangers to converse. Urban designers refer to this concept as triangulation. Conversation prompts promote CREs and is the idea behind Danish artist Jeppe Hein's "modified social benches" (4-10). His benches defy expectations of what a bench should be. They twist, contort, slant, droop, sag, curve, angle, and bend in a variety of shapes to provoke conversations among people who sit on them. Hein specifically designs these minimalist, galvanized steel

4-10

4-11

4-12

Connecting People

4-13

benches in basic white, black, or red to be sites of social interaction instead of places of rest and solitude. People are sitting and talking about his benches in France, Singapore, Spain, Germany, the United States and in temporary installations across three continents.

The proliferation of dog parks, such as the Patterson Dog Park in Baltimore, bring people together. Their four-legged companions provide the ideal conversation prompt that allow lite relationships to form (4-11). Surveys of dog park users in Georgia, Texas, and Florida have found that 80% of users see dog parks as a good way to meet neighbors and build a sense of community.

Shared Purpose

A sense of shared purpose contributes significantly to the creation of a CRE. Neighborhood tool libraries, where locals can borrow a variety of tools or specialized equipment for house maintenance, cooking, or gardening, provide a valuable community resource that brings neighbors together to share, discuss projects, and help each other. Staffed by volunteers, tool libraries typically request a donation and allow people to borrow items for a week. While the concept of community tool sharing is a very old one around the world, the term "tool library" popped up in Columbia, Ohio in the 1970s and the concept spread. Today one can find tool libraries as far flung as Britain, New Zealand, Slovenia, Sweden, and Canada – like this one in Toronto (4-12).

A sort of enhanced tool library, community "makerspaces" come in a variety of formats. In addition to tools or equipment, makerspaces also provide space for people to work in. Many offer training and workshops in specialized tools or techniques. For people whose home isn't amenable to welding, power tools, or 3-D printing, makerspaces provide a great resource. For those who just want to make things in a community setting, such as here in Urbana, Illinois, makerspaces provide a communication-rich, social gathering space (4-13).

In the mid-1990s Mark Lakeman traveled to Central America. Envious of how village residents would frequently gather around common spaces, he decided to bring that idea back to his hometown of Portland, Oregon. He started with one intersection in the Sellwood District, asking neighbors and ultimately city officials what they thought about designing and painting the intersection in bright colors. The neighbors loved the idea; the city did not and refused permission. It happened anyway. However, before sandblasting the paint away weeks later, annoyed city officials surveyed neighborhood residents who reported perceptions of less crime, slower traffic, and increased involvement in the neighborhood. The city acquiesced, and a community movement was born. Lakeman co-founded the

4-14

4-15

4-16

Connecting People

non-profit City Repair Project to help others brighten their neighborhoods through a shared purpose. The City of Portland, to its credit, embraced the concept and passed an ordinance allowing residents to apply for an "Intersection Repair" permit to temporarily close an intersection and paint it if enough area residents agree to the project. Jan Semenza, a professor of public health at Portland State University studied the impact of one painted intersection, the Sunnyside Piazza, finding that residents felt empowered. "It's not about the paint," reports Semenza, "it's about neighbors creating something bigger than themselves." The intersection projects build neighborhood relationships and provide a place gather beyond "painting day." Surrounding some of the now 38 painted intersections in the Portland area are community notice boards, tea stalls, chairs, "little free library" book exchanges, and playhouses. This good idea that has spread to other cities and countries (4-14).

Have some free wood? Need to borrow a ladder? Lost a dog? Have a recommendation for a plumber (4-15)? "Hyper-local" social networks represent another way to connect neighbors. For-profit companies such as Nextdoor and EveryBlock provide online platforms for neighborhood residents. They enforce basic policies to keep the conversations respectful and content focused on local-only information related to safety, goods, and services exchange, community-building, and projects or issues that directly affect that neighborhood. A user must live in the neighborhood and use their real name. Some of these sites allow police to post local crime updates or function as a news filter, posting stories relevant to the neighborhood. In contrast to larger social media sites, these hyper-local, online spaces link to a specific geographic neighborhood and often serve as a precursor to face-to-face interactions. When people come to pick up that lost dog, borrow the ladder, or purchase shelves they meet a new neighbor.

What better way to strengthen community connections than people coming together over the sharing of food? In Perth, Australia, the Twilight Hawker's Market celebrates that city's diversity through cuisine. Each summer this huge street food market offers a tour of Perth's international community. When launched in 2011, the diverse delights of international cuisine were virtually unknown to the typical resident. A few years later—judging by the lines at these vendor stalls—they can't get enough. Today,

4-17

local vendors represent over 30 countries, offering everything from Macedonian stuffed cabbage rolls, Greek wraps, South American cheese fingers, Indian doughnuts, paella, and more (4-16). Music and artisan goods complete the scene. As an added benefit, this Friday evening market takes place in what was an under-utilized city space called Forrest Place. A local organization, Events & Beyond, runs the successful Twilight Hawker's Market, hosted by Perth on city property.

In Portland, Oregon food trucks, appearing as shiny trucks, sheds on wheels, and hand painted campers have transformed how people eat and interact (4-17). At any given time, there are about 475 food carts or trucks open in downtown, as well as surrounding neighborhoods. Some cluster daily in the same "pods" with picnic tables nearby, while others roam the city, tweeting their locations. One can even take an organized Portland Food Cart Walking Tour. A study commissioned by the City of Portland found that food carts have a positive impact on street vitality and neighborhood life by promoting connectedness, distinctiveness, equity, and access. Portland food truck pods draw all income levels, cultures, ages, singles, and families. Not everyone is in favor of food trucks. Restaurants with their high rents and expensive capital improvements believe that food trucks are taking away business and are beginning to mobilize to limit the amount or locations of food trucks. Despite the critics, food truck clusters offer a new form of CRE. Interactions are informal and relaxed. There are places to sit and converse. Food is a terrific conversation prompt. It's fluid—people come and go—and for a shared purpose: to eat.

Strive for Distinctiveness

In their book *Future Forms and Design for Sustainable Cities*, Mike Jenks and Nicola Dempsey state emphatically that place matters. Sense of place is what makes one city different from another based on its distinctive profile of human, cultural, historical, and natural characteristics. We know that a harbor city is different from a mountain city or plains city or desert city not just in climate, but in the layout of the streets, the look of the buildings, the foods that are traditional, the plants growing in the gardens, and even the times of the year that are important or special to people. When we are in a distinctive city, or neighborhood, we know where we are. Most critical, is that pride in a place's positive distinctiveness is what motivates people to care and make good choices about where they live.

For some cities, however, cultivating a distinctive sense of place isn't easy. After a near century of suburbanization, and now globalization, not all cities possess distinctive qualities anymore. In her 1961 book *The Death and Life of Great American Cities* journalist, activist, and urban observer Jane Jacobs argued that modernizing cities are "losing their memories." She admonished the urban planners of the time who were creating concrete malls, freeways, and tract home sameness, that erased historical architecture and unique ecological systems alike. Authors such as Jenks and Dempsey argue that globalized design and city "branding" campaigns diminish a city's character and individuality. This commodification of cities in turn weakens community pride because of a lack of positive distinctiveness.

It turns out that cities with a strong sense of place exhibit certain qualities that really connect people to their city. Knowing these qualities can help other cities, or neighborhoods, develop their own strategies for enhancing community pride.

Know your DNA

First, cities with a strong sense of place recognize and prioritize their distinctive elements of place. Suzanne Crowhurst Lennard, founder and director of International Making Cities Livable organization, refers to this as the DNA of a city. For some cities, it's found in a historic and iconic connection to the past, such as in Rome or Athens. For other cities it revolves around a natural feature, such as the canals in Bruges, Belgium or the hilltop location of Orvieto, Italy. A city's identity might relate to a product or art or industry such as opera in Lucca; the jasmine smells of Grasse, France, the perfume capital of the world; or the pugnacious scent of Gilroy, California, the garlic capital of the world. In these cases residents

4-18

are proud of, and feel connected to, that distinctive aspect of their home and celebrate them through festivals and events, such as the popular Gilroy Garlic Festival (4-18). (Yes, they serve garlic ice cream.) The DNA of other places might relate more to lifestyle attributes, such as the tapas scene in San Sebastian, Spain or the spiritual mecca of the red rocks of Sedona, Arizona.

Cities seeking to reimagine, restore or reinvigorate a city or neighborhood's sense of place should turn, not to advertisers, but to their residents, asking what they perceive as the most important assets, elements, and stories of place. Those residents might emphasize the smell of pine trees, the architecture of old houses, or the diversity of neighborhoods. Such input offers valuable clues for city planners concerned with strengthening a city's sense of place.

In surveys, it is most common for residents of cities—regardless of size, prosperity, and geography—to mention some aspect of nature as a key asset. The lesson here is for cities to prioritize views, trees, and parks, and to daylight buried streams or rivers, reclaim industrial waterfronts, and build networks of greenways that showcase the natural environment.

Once covered completely with concrete highways in the frenzy of post Korea-war economic development (4-19), a massive and expensive urban

Connecting People

4-19

4-20

renewal project restored Cheonggyecheon Stream in Seoul, South Korea. Reopened in 2005, the ambitious project sought to re-introduce nature to the city, as well restore part of Seoul's history and culture. (The Stream's original beauty had beckoned the king of the Choson Dynasty, 14C–19C, to erect a new capital at the site.) The project daylighted 3.6 miles of the stream, brought back the natural plants and habitat that surrounded it, and added pedestrian trails and bridges to reconnect people to this incredible natural asset (4-20). While criticized for its high price tag (and the fact that some of the water comes through pipes from the Han River) the stream is now extremely popular and well used, with estimates ranging from 64,000 to 90,000 pedestrians each day visiting and walking its shoreline paths. The benefits of this massive undertaking have been many. In addition to connecting people to nature, there is a 600% increase in the number native species of birds, fish, and insects, an improvement in air quality (more plants, fewer cars, more breeze through the corridor), a reduction in the urban heat island effect along the stream (summer air temperatures are five degrees cooler than surrounding areas), a residential and business revitalization of the areas along the Cheonggyecheon, and a bridging of the north-south dividing line that the highways created. It also had the unexpected effect of speeding up traffic around the city, despite removal of the highways.

4-21

4-22

4-23

4-24

Respect the old and integrate the new

A city with a strong sense of place accepts, embraces, and honors its history, then integrates that past with its present and evolving future. One of the best examples of this integration is Berlin. Dozens of significant monuments, museums, and memorials tie Berlin's urban landscape to its tumultuous past, from the Brandenburg Gate to the Memorial to the Murdered Jews of Europe (4-21) to remnants from the Berlin Wall (4-22) and many more historic sites. In fact, the Berlin Wall came down so quickly in the joy of that defining moment that some Berliners now worry there isn't enough of it left to serve as a cultural and historical reminder. Berlin's unique sense of place arises from the combination of these historical symbols with prolific markers of life, growth, and youth. Berlin boasts plenty of parks, green space, squares, trees, wide streets, charming neighborhoods, artist studios, and a vibrantly young population (4-23).

It took 20 years to build the Three Rivers Heritage Trail in Pittsburgh. What began as an effort to reclaim the polluted, and economically dying, industrial waterfront for public use developed into a defining feature for a city that is proud of its history. Twenty-two miles (with more miles planned) attract over one million users a year with trails that run along both sides of three rivers and weave through ten neighborhoods of Pittsburgh. The 185 miles of waterway, with 23 kayak and canoe access points, is one of the best urban water trails in the United States. The Three Rivers Heritage Trail project restored abandoned bridges for modern use, while preserving the unique historical details of each bridge. For example, the abandoned Hot Metal Bridge that used to carry molten iron from furnaces on the north to the south side of the Mononghala River (4-24) is now a pedestrian and bicycle bridge. Historical interpretive markers along this rails-to-trails project allow visitors to visualize Pittsburgh's past with images of the original natural settings, juxtaposed with photos of the iron furnaces and steel factories that once fueled Pittsburgh's economy.

Of course, a city's distinctive elements may evolve over time, reflecting changing conditions and community members. Malmo, Sweden had a proud 300-year shipbuilding heritage, but eventually lost the industry in a very short time to South Korea. It was a sad day for the former shipyard workers, who donned their work uniforms, and went to the harbor to wave goodbye to largest shipbuilding crane in the world as it left for Korea. Although residents of Malmo hoped that the industrial jobs would return, the mayor of the city, Ilmar Reepalu, believed it was time for Malmo to create a new identity for itself based on knowledge, modern architecture, culture, and green technology. A new downtown university brought younger people into the city center. The Swedish Green Roof Institute now attracts people from all over the world to learn about green roofs and natural stormwater management. These steps, and others, launched a new

4-26

4-27

4-25

4-28

4-29

future for the city. However, to bridge the past, present and future The Turning Torso, an iconic residential and office tower designed by Santiago Calatrava, rose close to where the tallest shipbuilding crane stood. Now the tallest building in northern Europe, The Turning Torso symbolizes a new and different Malmo, but with a respectful nod to its past (4-25).

Another way that cities integrate the past and present is through innovative, adaptive re-use of historical buildings. In Copenhagen, the former Holman naval base hangar, built in 1921 to house reconnaissance planes, provides an inspiring setting for the Royal Danish Academy of Fine Arts architecture students (4-26, 4-27).

Connecting People

4-30　　　　　　　　　　　　4-31

When Copenhagen and Malmo combined their ports as part of the creation of the Oresund Region, they repurposed the industrial waterfront for residential and commercial use by both cities. In part of the docklands area in Copenhagen sat, for over 60 years, two large concrete seed silos built during World War II. Rather than tearing them down and creating tons of landfill waste, the massive concrete structures became the bones for two new apartment buildings, the Gemini Apartments (4-28). In an innovative design approach, the Dutch architects MVRDV chose to place the apartments around, rather than inside, the silos because cutting windows, doors, and other openings into the concrete would compromise the integrity of the structure. A translucent plastic ceiling above the silos provides natural light to the interior of the innovative structure where the stairway and elevators are located. Also shown here, a bike and pedestrian path is the fastest way for residents to get to the shopping area.

Smaller city scenes might also connect people with their city's past. Underground metro and train stations often have a huge amount of unused space. Riders are a captive audience who appreciate having something interesting to look at rather than advertisements or blank concrete walls. Some cities turn subway stops into venues for showcasing history. At Mexico City's Zócalo transit station there is a scale model of the Templo Mayor pyramid from the ancient Tenochtitlan city (4-29).

Gnomes reside all over the Polish city of Wroclaw guarding spaces, passed out drunk, waving, juggling, dancing, asleep in a tiny bed, riding a horse, pushing balls (4-30), or chained to a window bar as if in jail (4-31) among other amusing or serious antics. The city publishes maps so visitors can locate these unique tiny residents of this city, but these tourists often do so oblivious to the gnomes' historical significance. For residents, the gnomes tell a story of Wroclaw's turbulent history and contribute to a strong sense of place. Poland, along with many Slavic cultures, has a rich folklore of gnomes, dwarves, and elves. But under repressive and authoritarian rule, gnomes became a symbol of the dissident movement (the Orange Alternative) in part, because they had no strong political connotation. Activists painted them on walls during the 1980s as part of a movement to stage absurdist and nonsensical actions that demonstrated, in a peaceful yet subversive way, the absurd actions of an authoritarian government that under martial law had stripped people of their rights. And indeed, it was humiliating for officials to be seen painting over the cute little guys – or to arrest activists gathering peacefully while dressed in tall, orange felt gnome hats. After the fall of communism in 1989 the gnomes remained an important symbol of political freedom in Wroclaw. In 2001 the installation of the tiny gnomes began first as a tribute to the Orange Alternative protests, then as symbols of a broader range of human rights, including for women and the disabled. Current figures put Wroclaw's proud gnome population at 300.

With horses or horse-drawn carriages the primary mode of transportation in the early 1900s, iron or brass horse rings began to appear on the sidewalks of Portland and were soon in abundance across the city. With the advent of cars, the city began to remove the rings when repair or new construction took place. That is, until 1978 when a Portland resident complained about the disappearing rings and the loss of the Portland's history. The city changed course, deciding to maintain or replace the rings. Fast forward to 2005. Resident Scott Wayne Indiana wanted his neighbors to notice these small artifacts of Portland history. So, he tethered a plastic horse to an iron horse ring in the Pearl District. Soon after, "The Horse Project" took off. People started to tether toy horses (sometimes accompanied by saddles, hay, and lassoes) to rings around the city to the delight of residents and visitors (4-32). While Portland is a city with a strong sense of place due to many qualities, the horse rings and the whimsical following they generate is another point of pride, and personality, for this distinctive city.

Support unique cultural practices

Social rituals, cultural practices, or unique and festive events also act as important markers of community identity. These activities might celebrate

4-32

local history, cuisine, harvests, or lifestyle. Whether it's the annual cheese-rolling event in Cooper's Hill, England or the San Francisco Pride Parade, such events play an important role in maintaining a sense of place in any size community.

Spain probably boasts the greatest number of unusual cultural events historically linked to the identity of it towns. There's the annual tomato fight, La Tomatina, in Buñol, Valencia; the Baby Jumping (El Colacho) holiday in Castrillo de Murcia (4-33); The Running of the Bulls (most famous in Pamplona); the Near Death Experience event (part of the Fiesta de Santa Marta de Ribarteme) in Las Nieves, Galicia; and many more. Most Catalonians have attended a Castellers (human towers) contest (4-34). The rhythms of daily life stop to celebrate these experiences so integral to the history and identity of place.

Cities should also support neighborhood distinctiveness. The Powderhorn 24 is a bike event intended to celebrate the special character and strong community spirit of the racially and economically diverse neighborhood of

4-33

4-34

4-35

4-36

Connecting People

Powderhorn in South Minneapolis (4-35). Riders, many in costume or with decorated bikes, ride laps around and within the neighborhood stopping at a series of checkpoints to get their "manifest" punched to record the laps completed. (The most ambitious riders can cover up to 400 miles.) At some checkpoints, riders engage in some community task, such as helping put mulch on a garden or participating in a yoga class at the neighborhood park. In fact, respect of the community is paramount. If a rider is disrespectful in any way, they must complete a "dunce lap" to apologize to every checkpoint captain. If not riding, plenty of residents pull up lawn chairs, offer water and food, and generally come out to cheer their fun-loving neighbors on bikes.

The Jaimanitas neighborhood near Havana, Cuba has been rechristened Fusterlandia for a good reason. Ceramist Jose Fuster has covered not only his own home and studio with colorful mosaics, but also the homes of his neighbors and even the local medical clinic (4-36). Fuster hired many neighbors, particularly youth, to continue his artistic vision (and economic boost) for this neighborhood. Jaimanitas mosaics create a neighborhood identity distinct from any other in the world.

Promote authentic placemaking

Developing a sense of place is not just defining boundaries and attaching a name to it. People need to emotionally connect to a place. For this reason, community organizers advocate the recognition of "naturally occurring" clusters of urban activity, rather than the invention of places using real estate market-driven names. For example, the idea of Naturally Occurring Cultural Districts (NORDs) embodies a more authentic approach to the identification of clusters of cultural activity in a city. Advocates argue that cultural districts within a city should arise more organically around areas where artists, cultural organizations, and creative industries tend to cluster rather than only describe the space around large museums or theaters. In much the same way that Naturally Occurring Retirement Communities (NORCs)—a term recognized by the U.S. federal government since 1986— become eligible for services and funding once demographic criteria are met, similar policies can develop around cultural or other types of unique districts. This process of forming NORCs, found in parts of New York City, Baltimore, Philadelphia, and Tucson, encourages a stronger sense of place

4-37   4-38

and connection among those who live and work there. The Fourth Arts Block is a NORC in New York City that is home to an array of cultural groups, artists, and performance festivals such as one called "Meet the Streets" shown here (4-37).

Although custom-made street furnishings such as these bike racks in the neighborhood of Adams Morgan cost more, they can represent an authentic link to the area's proud multicultural history as a gateway for immigrants to Washington, D.C. (4-38) For residents in the know, the name represents the symbolic "merger" of two formerly segregated elementary schools (one black, one white) following the 1954 Bolling v. Sharpe Supreme Court ruling that the segregation of D.C. schools was unconstitutional. Soon thereafter, the Adams Morgan Community Council formed, paving the way in the 1960s for the creation of a new elementary school and community center complex open to all. While over the years, Adam Morgan has seen significant gentrification, rising housing costs, and a weekend influx of partiers for its nightlife, the residents are proud of the name on that bike rack sign, symbolizing a multicultural history and independent neighborhood character.

Support local storytellers
At the local level, many actors contribute to a sense of place: local historians, bloggers, librarians, artists, as well as neighborhood groups and non-profits. In Seattle, one can find a long list of neighborhood blogs at the city website. Several cities have also launched the newest trend in promoting

4-39

community connection: hyper-local radio stations. These FCC-approved low-power radio stations (they use about the same amount of power as a 100-watt bulb) have a 3.5 to 5-mile radius – just enough to cover a handful of neighborhoods. While these tiny radio stations can stream online, their goal is to connect people in a neighborhood. Volunteers for hyper-local radio stations, such as one in Rainier Valley, Seattle (4-39), hope to explore local music, social causes, lifestyles, hobbies, food, community news, and politics through the voices of their neighbors.

Non-profit organizations also tell a city's stories through the issues they promote. Feet First, based in Seattle, promotes walking for health, safety, a better environment, and social connection. One of the organization's most popular programs is Walking Ambassadors. Trained volunteers lead neighborhood walks so residents of all ages can explore, share knowledge, meet new neighbors, and connect more closely with the unique sights and smells of each neighborhood all the while improving their health by walking (4-40). The Walking Ambassadors offer some neighborhood history, provide tidbits about local public art and architecture, and draw attention to a neighborhood's trees, birds, and geology. The organization also produces free neighborhood walking maps.

4-40

4-41

When connecting people to their city, no community group or their history should be left out. Know Your City is a unique nonprofit based in Portland, Oregon that "engages the public in art and social justice through creative placemaking projects." Through tours, publications, lectures, and youth programs the organization makes the "histories and cultures of ALL Oregonians" come alive. One tour is called "A People's History of Portland." It's walking route and narrative celebrate the immigrant and working-class roots of the city, including the story of Portland's Chinese population (4-41).

Many cities host amateur photo contests to tell a city's stories and enhance a sense of place. Some cities divide contests into categories such as people, community events, wildlife and nature, and city landmarks, ensuring plenty of photographic reminders of what people love about their city. Others, like The Best of Davis photo contest, asks residents to submit photos of "anything that embodies the spirit of what living in Davis means" – like the beauty of stargazing on a clear night (4-42).

Connecting people is to build social capital through the promotion of communication-rich environments. Connecting people is also the promotion of a city's assets and distinctive identity in ways that enhance an authentic sense of place and community pride. When people feel connection, they are more willing to work together in good and bad times. The result is a more resilient and socially sustainable city.

4-42

5/

Communicating with People

The scientific evidence is alarming. Humans are exceeding and eroding Earth's carrying capacity. We are not living within our means. Due to overconsumption and population growth, the planet is on track to run out of accessible, non-renewable resources such as coal, oil, and gas. And, if we don't change how we manage renewable resources—such as water, wood, and fish—they will essentially become non-renewable as well. Add to this pollution and human contributions to climate change, and the need for change is both urgent and clear. Cities cannot rely on national governments to spearhead meaningful change. They need to aggressively confront these challenges through laws, policies, commitment to research and development, prioritization of resources, and courageous leadership at all levels.

But cities need something else. They need citizens who embrace new ways of doing things. They need citizens willing to interact responsibly with their environment and support city actions to do so as well. Even the most charismatic city leadership can't just tell people what to do and expect change. They must educate, engage, and collaborate with people so they make informed decisions, express their ideas and aspirations, and take actions that are good for them and for their community.

Educate. Engage. Collaborate. This chapter highlights some communication strategies known to be effective in overcoming public resistance to change and in motivating people to engage in ways that will improve their communities.

Take it to the Streets

One of the best ways to raise awareness and educate people is to go where they are – on the streets and in their neighborhoods.

Start with a Taste Test

One strategy for encouraging community members, city officials, or business owners to embrace change is to test new ideas in real life settings. We're not talking about expensive, grand urban experiments, but rather the opposite: small scale, short term, low cost, low risk, and potentially high reward tests of different ways of doing something. This strategy appears under various names, such as pilot tests, demonstration projects, tactical urbanism, DIY urbanism, pop-up urbanism, or "living labs." But the purpose is the same. Tests as a communication strategy are an effective way to change attitudes in the face of skepticism or misinformation and, on a practical level, help cities to see if design or programmatic ideas will work before making any substantial investments.

For example, tests offer an excellent way to assess the feasibility of pedestrian malls. Popular pedestrian areas such as the Strøget in Copenhagen or Times Square in New York City began with pilot tests. Mexico City employed this approach with Calle Francisco I. Madero (or Madero Street), a road stretching through the historic city center. For years, pedestrians crowded narrow sidewalks next to an unhealthy jam of cars (5-1). In 2009 the mayor proposed to permanently close four blocks of the busy street from the central square into the downtown and re-route traffic, but there was strong opposition from small businesses and skeptical citizens. In a compromise, the mayor proposed a 3-month test, blocking Madero Street only on Mondays. The city worked with businesses to measure the effect of that first test. After two weeks, businesses agreed to expand the test to include Mondays and Tuesdays. After three months, based on enthusiastic feedback of citizens and local businesses, the results were in. Existing businesses were thriving, as more people than ever came to stroll, linger, and

5-1   5-2   5-3

shop along this historic street. Soon the street became permanently closed to cars. Many new businesses have opened and real estate values increased – along with air quality. To further improve this popular pedestrian mall the city repaved the street, eliminating the curb that separated people from cars, and added benches and landscaping (5-2).

Some bike-lane projects begin as demonstration projects using temporary materials to direct and redirect bikes and traffic. City officials learn from these short-term tests by monitoring use and getting community feedback before deciding whether and how to move forward with the project. Equally important, the public acclimates to the idea of new bike lanes and changed traffic patterns. Shown here is a test of a proposed bike lane on Seattle's 2nd Avenue (5-3).

A sleepy and underutilized public square, London's Guildhall Yard became a "chair bombing" test site. For one month, the city installed 100 movable chairs to see if this change would give life to the space. Within a few days a lunchtime crowd occupied nearly all the chairs, creating a friendly and relaxed atmosphere (5-4). After completion of the test and removal of the chairs, the public asked for them back on a permanent basis along with some tables and a coffee stall.

On the other hand, in another small experiment in London, the city placed a small patch of green lawn in an awkward void of a small public plaza (5-5). Would the grass attract people? It didn't. People continued to avoid the little area, so the city abandoned the idea. In this case, the city saved thousands of dollars on a permanent lawn installation for the plaza by purchasing only a few rolls of test grass.

Cities also test new technologies, such as how pedestrians, cyclists, and

5-4   5-5

motorists react to different types of smart road crossings. Smart crossings combine sensors, cameras, LED lights, and, in some cases, computer neural networks, to assess the number and speed of pedestrians at a crossing and adjust the walk and traffic signals accordingly. Some smart crosswalks, such as this one tested in Mitcham, south London, use technology that replaces asphalt with a nonslip surface that can light up and flash messages to cars, bicyclists, and pedestrians to confirm safe, or warn of dangerous, passage (5-6). Some smart crosswalks can change color, shape, size, and even direction to adapt to the trajectory a rushed or smartphone-distracted pedestrian might take across the street.

5-6

Stage Public Events

The first step toward change is to raise awareness of a problem and its possible solutions. Staging large scale events or installations that alter public spaces is a powerful type of communication strategy because the event looms large, and its message becomes a social and educational experience shared by many people.

To prepare Parisians for a city with fewer cars and better air, starting in 2015, the city launched the idea of "A Day without Cars" in the center

5-7

5-8

5-9

5-10

of the city (5-7). This event serves as part logistical experiment for the city and part awareness raising for the public. For the 2017 event, Paris closed an unprecedented 40 square miles of the city to all but emergency vehicles, taxis, and buses from 11am to 6pm on a Sunday, encouraging Parisians to walk, bike, rollerblade, shift their attitudes, and move a little slower.

Linda Tegg designed her large-scale Grasslands installation in Melbourne, Australia to raise awareness about urban development and the loss the city's connection to the local ecosystem. Tegg spent over two years reading indigenous and settlers' records. She also worked with botanists to research the natural habitat and species once part of the original landscape and now covered in concrete. Then, she installed over 10,000 of those native plants to create an urban retreat in front of the main Melbourne library as part of a week-long Melbourne International Arts Festival in 2014 (5-8). The profound impact and popularity of the event brought calls from local citizens to make the installation permanent.

Another example of an awareness building event that alters public spaces is International Park[ing] Day (5-9). On one day a year, community groups can turn on-street parking spaces into temporary public parks by creating parklets. Originating in San Francisco, this event quickly went viral around the world and led to the development of parklets programs in many cities. Park[ing] Day not only gets people to rethink how we use streets, but shows the storefront businesses adjacent to these parklets that public spaces, however small, activate and attract people in ways that can enhance their businesses.

The Trash Fashion Bash Holiday Explosion, produced by i-SUSTAIN and put on at the Seattle Art Museum, was a fun way to communicate about how much extra waste the holiday season generates. The elegant cocktail dress shown here is 100% department store plastic bags knitted together (5-10). While not held in an outdoor public space, this event garnered a lot of local media attention for its very creative theme.

Send Real-Time Messages

One significant barrier to changing behaviors is the concept of *cognitive distance*. To many people, the problems of climate change and resource degradation seem amorphous and distant. Most people do not actually see melting glaciers, depleted forests, or polluted watersheds. So, when encouraged to switch to LED lights, take the bus more often, or try meat-free Mondays people can feel a disconnect between those actions and the larger issues they help to mitigate. There is also distance in time. When scientists speak of the critical changes coming by the end of this century, that's a nanosecond in Earth calculations. For the rest of us, it is beyond our lifetimes.

Real-time messaging is a communication strategy that tries to educate or encourage behaviors at a point of decision making, interest, or opportunity. This sign in Melbourne lets people know that their litter ends up in the city's river (5-11). Real-time messaging is also effective anywhere people might pause, such as waiting to cross the street, as seen in this small sign embedded next to a stormwater drain (5-12). Another approach is to place signage in unexpected places. This sign inside the Longford, Ireland cemetery surprises visitors with a message about life and biodiversity (5-13).

Sometimes people just need a little real-time nudge to engage in healthier behaviors. In 2012, Matt Tomasulo, a graduate student in urban planning at the University of North Carolina, put up 27 signs at three intersections in Raleigh during the night. As part of his master's thesis, Tomasulo was testing ways to encourage people to walk more. The signs announce the time it takes to walk to a destination, along with QR codes so pedestrians can download directions on their smartphones. The vinyl, weatherproof signs used a simple color scheme to designate the type of destination – for example, green for parks. The walking distances were short. The signs lasted almost a month before the city took them down. It took a month because the signs were so professional-looking that city officials assumed someone had authorized them. However, by that time, Tomasulo's Walk Raleigh project received media exposure and local supporters collected 1,300 signatures in three days asking the city council to approve the return of the signs. Success! The city let the signs go back up for a sanctioned test this time: a 90-day pilot program. Again, success. After the pilot test, people reported that the signs

5-11   5-12

5-13   5-14

motivated them to walk. Soon other cities were contacting Tomasulo—from Germany, France, Great Britain, and elsewhere in the U.S.—wanting to do something similar. Armed with the positive feedback and some Kickstarter money, Tomasulo launched Walk [Your City]. The organization offers customized sign templates now seen in more than 100 cities around the world. Here's an example found as part of Walk San Jose (5-14).

Another type of real-time messaging tells people that what they do matters. One example is the bicycle counters found in several cities around the world, such as this one in Copenhagen (5-15). As each cyclist rides by, sensors update the digital display to announce how many cyclists have ridden this stretch that day, that week, or over the year. Some counters display target numbers so cyclists feel like they are contributing to a specific community goal. Bicycle counters provide several benefits for a city trying to lower its carbon emissions while promoting personal health.

5-15   5-16

The first benefit is to bring more attention to bicycling as a viable means of transportation. The second benefit is motivational. By counting cyclists, it tells them they are important. Third, the data collected helps a city develop its multimodal transportation system. In the U.S. Seattle, then Portland were first to install bicycle counters. Other cities have followed.

Let People Decide

Oftentimes it is the city officials that need to learn from the public. Initiatives such as Airports to Parks allow residents to propose how to use a space, then the city responds. In Berlin, an old airport closed leaving a large barren site, Tempelhofer Feld, full of runways and land adjacent to the original airport terminal. While the city sponsored a design competition for how to renovate and reuse the terminal, it let the community experiment with different approaches for what to do with the field. To facilitate this, the city designated Tempelhofer Feld a "temporary" park space, providing citizens information about the land and its native ecology. The space became a blank canvas. People tried out a variety of uses. They rode bikes and skateboards on runways, built community gardens, staged public art displays, held kite flying events, and more (5-16). The results informed the city and community as to the best future use of this historic airport space. The fate of closed airports in Chang Rai, Thailand; Quinta, Ecuador; New York City; Frankfurt, Germany; and Santa Monica, California have used similar community-driven approaches.

In the seaside town of Brighton, England a long street called New Road had, over many years, lost any local appeal, serving primarily as a somewhat hostile thoroughfare for cars. Residents avoided its narrow

5-17

and obstacle-ridden sidewalks despite its central location in the city. City officials researched options of how to revitalize New Road. Should they upgrade the sidewalks, but keep the road for cars? Should the street become a long pedestrian mall? Should it become a transit only road? In the end the city decided to create the physical framework, then let people decide. The city repaved the road with attractive natural stone, eliminated sidewalk curbs to widen the space and allow pedestrians to walk anywhere, and installed several amenities such as benches, better lighting, and bike racks. Here's the twist. The road was open to everyone with no rules as to its use. There were no painted lines to guide people, bikes, or cars. There were no speed limit signs. New Road, completed in 2005, became England's first "shared space" street. And, instead of creating a chaotic and dangerous street, it turned out that pedestrians and bikes just took control, significantly slowing the movement of any cars down the road. Today, New Road and businesses along it are thriving. It is a much-used, multi-use shared— and extremely safe—street space (5-17).

Motivate People to Engage

Community engagement is essential to creating livable and sustainable cities. Cities need people to roll up their sleeves and volunteer time, ideas, and effort to help make their neighborhood or city a better one. Here is a committed team of volunteers planting trees in Yerevan, Armenia (5-18).

5-18

For cities, the co-benefits of community engagement far outweigh the challenges:

Resources and talent. Volunteers help cities leverage limited resources, in both staff and money.

Everyone learns. Involving people educates a city about its residents' needs and desires, as well as residents about the issues and constraints faced by their city.

Innovation. Projects that involve community members benefit from diverse perspectives, knowledge, and skills.

Commitment. When people invest time in their community, it strengthens their level of commitment.

Relationships. Community engagement is about building relationships, not just between city officials and residents, but among residents. When volunteers come together to work on shared community goals, it fosters the kind of lite relationships that build social capital.

Authentic and lasting change. Improvements that result from bottom-up versus top-down processes tend to last because the changes more authentically reflect what a community wants and needs.

So, what motivates people to get involved? Psychologists, and seasoned community leaders, will point to a short list of essentials that are critical for cities to understand. The first three cluster together: *positive identity*, *camaraderie*, and *values alignment*. People like to share positive experiences as part of a group that, in their view, is doing something that aligns with their values. People also seek a sense of *personal efficacy* (I did this!) and *group identity* (We did this!), like to *learn new things*, and will continue their involvement if they see tangible *outcomes and impact*. Finally, most people like to receive some *acknowledgment* for their knowledge, efforts, and talents.

Traditional tools for community engagement have been public opinion surveys, town halls, or public meetings. These tools have real limitations, in large part, because they don't feed that short list of motivations for positive engagement. Instead, they tend to attract the same narrow range of people and limit real dialogue. Today, we see cities use more creative tools for involving the community.

Invite the Community to Collect Data

Citizen science is an engagement technique that takes advantage of all the key motivators. The basic idea is that citizens collect large amounts of data from many locations that scientists or cities simply cannot afford to do. Volunteers get some training and learn new things. Participants feel part of a team with a broader purpose. Their contribution, large or small, makes a difference. The projects typically have a fixed duration and outcome, and participants can devote as much or as little time as they want (this is important).

While we might envision people recording observations in forests or at beaches, citizen science is also a terrific technique for collecting data within cities. Melbourne's BioBlitz was a great example of a successful, citywide, citizen-science project (5-19). The city wanted to improve its knowledge of local biodiversity. So, during 15 days in spring, 700 citizens

5-19

5-20

volunteered and collected over 3,000 records of insects, plants, mammals, reptiles, birds, fungi, and fish. Volunteers even discovered some rare and new species not previously known to be in area. To make the BioBlitz accessible to all, volunteers could use a variety of tools depending on their assignment, interests, and abilities. Options included recording information using Instagram, Twitter, web entry, handwritten sightings, photos, or smartphone apps. Organizers provided participants with an easy-to-follow toolkit and a way to ask questions. The response was terrific. Eager to participate, people of all ages learned a lot about the biodiversity of their city (and threats to it) in the process.

Other types of citizen science projects employ sensor technologies attached to volunteers' smartphones or tablets. As volunteers go about the day, they record data (or perceptions) of urban attributes such as noise levels or air quality for scientists to then correlate with other types of data (such as traffic or weather patterns).

A nearly-year long city project called "Community Character in a Box" in Austin, Texas employed another approach to community-based data collection. For this project, neighbors formed teams to investigate their own neighborhood. The city organizers provided a do-it-yourself kit—yes, literally a box—to guide neighborhood groups through a process where they mapped, photographed, discussed, and defined the unique character of their neighborhoods (5-20). The kit instructions posed questions such as: What are the most important cultural, historical, or unique spaces in your neighborhood? Where do you like to hang out or meet people? Show us what you are most proud of? Where are the problems? What needs improvement? Each team returned the maps, photos and descriptions to city staff. Over 100 Austin neighborhoods turned in boxes of insights, based on thousands of volunteer hours. As a final step, the city hosted neighborhood workshops to allow participants to talk about what they discovered about the character of their neighborhood. The workshops helped prioritize ideas for city action, as well as provide critical input to the city for updating land use and environmental codes.

5-21

Hold a Contest

The staging of contests can be a great way to get people, of all ages, involved in community improvement. For example, several cities have hosted contests for filling "urban voids" – those small, awkward, or underused spaces on city property. Brighton, Colorado hosts an annual "Big Little Idea Contest." Teams submit ideas to make "Brighten a better place to live, learn, work, and play." Six winning teams get $500 each and permission to install their project. Other cities sponsor contests for creative designs for bus stops, solar lighting, railroad underpass art, or, in Omaha, for the creative repurposing of grain elevators. Staging a contest is great, but the real success of this technique is the motivator of tangible outcomes – the winning entry must happen. For example, the Portland Department of Transportation hosted a contest to come up with designs for symbols on city bike paths. Participants submitted their entries by age group. Here the winner from primary school is getting her design, "Singing Bicycle" painted on a Portland bike lane (5-21). What a thrill for Vivian.

5-22

5-23

5-24

Another type of contest seeks to change people's behavior. Two organizations, Hubbub and CommonWorks, collaborated to launch a campaign called "Neat Streets" in London. One of the campaign targets was to tackle the large quantity of cigarette butts littering public spaces, a known environmental hazard that leaches toxins into soils and water. They came up with a clever contest idea: Vote your Butt. The organizers placed shallow display boxes around the city asking people to vote on different sports questions using a cigarette butt. (Sports topics attracted the most people.) The voting station shown here asked people to vote on whether Ronaldo or Messi is the best soccer/football player in the world (5-22) ... and cleared the area of harmful cigarette butts.

Sponsor (Free) Classes

Most people love to learn, and to get things for free, so put them together to offer free classes on topics such as creating a front yard rain garden or lowering one's energy bill. In Copenhagen, where bicycling is so much part of the culture, the Danish Red Cross teaches free classes to newcomers, such as immigrants and refugees. Participants in these popular classes are often older women from countries where women do not traditionally ride bikes. They learn techniques for safe cycling and basic bike repair (5-23). They also gain confidence, a low cost means of transportation, and a way to participate in this integral aspect of Danish life.

Speak to Local Identity

In Billings, Montana the city started a clever, and very effective, program to encourage certain (not so tidy) neighborhoods to participate in a city-sponsored cleanup of litter, abandoned junk, and weeds gone wild. They named the program: I Got A TUNE UP (5-24). The slogan spoke directly to Billings' residents long time love of classic cars. Neighborhoods that participated in the clean-up received signs, stickers, and t-shirts with the I Got A TUNE UP slogan and, once spruced up, a neighborhood party sponsored by the city.

Make it Easy with Technology

Even a normally apathetic or time-stressed resident might whip out a smartphone to report a bad pothole. The proliferation of city-sponsored smartphone apps is another community engagement trend. People can report potholes, dead streetlights, abandoned furniture, graffiti, and other non-emergency problems (5-25). Mobile app platforms adopted by cities such as SeeClickFix, FixMyStreet, CitySourced, or Find it Fix it take advantage of technologies such as GPS locating, Google maps, smartphone cameras, and texting to make it easy for a person to take and upload a picture that shows a problem. The city can immediately see and locate even a pothole using GPS coordinates. Cities that prioritize these app notifications clearly benefit. It not only improves the city streets and services, but quick responses build trust and support between the city and its citizens. And, as just suggested, it's a strategy that engages a broader range of people in improving their community, such as those who love to complain but would never take the time to volunteer.

5-25

Cities also use online platforms such as Give a Minute,

5-26

5-27

Road open for people!

Neighborland, or Citizenspace to collect opinions, ideas, or engage in conversations on specific topics or general queries. Using this approach, city agencies can ask citizens to just "give a minute" to post their thoughts by text message, Twitter, Facebook, or at a website. For example, Give A Minute Chicago posed this question to residents: "Hey Chicago, what would encourage you to walk, bike, and take the CTA more often?" The messages and responses appear at a central, online project space in the form of virtual post-it notes for anyone to view. This makes people's input accessible to city agencies, non-profits, civic groups, and citizens themselves. To encourage participation, a large advertising campaign accompanied the roll out of Give a Minute Chicago.

Employ the Language of Change

Many years ago, David C. Korten wrote a powerful essay in *Yes!* magazine titled "Change the Story, Change the Future." Korten argued that *how* we talk about issues, the stories and language we use, can place constraints on our ability to enact change. Others have also argued this same point. Albert Einstein famously said, "We cannot solve our problems with the same thinking we used when we created them."

George Ferguson, the former mayor of Bristol, UK agrees that language matters. In one small, but powerful example, he introduced a program in Bristol called 'Make Sunday Special' where neighborhood groups host a community activity, such as a festival, dance party, or kid's play on their street. City transportation officials, accordingly, placed "Road Closed"

5-28

signs up for the first Sunday events (5-26). The mayor would have none of it. Within two weeks, new signs appeared that said "Road Open for People!" (5-27). It's a mindset, Ferguson argues. We just assume that streets are only for cars. We must change our language, to change our future.

Collaborate Across Sectors

To effect lasting and positive change at all levels of community life cities must creatively partner with all sectors – nonprofit, academic, business, and citizen. Cross-sector collaboration makes sense not just from a resource perspective, but each sector contributes complementary strengths.

Ask Citizens to be Owners

Samsø is a small island off the coast of Denmark with lots of potatoes. Today it is also a model renewable energy community with 100% of its electricity coming from wind power, bringing new jobs, businesses, and international interest. It still has a lot of potato farmers, but they are also proud owners nine of the 11 onshore wind turbines on the island (5-28). But, for Soren

Hermansen, it was a tough sell. A local farmer and teacher, Hermansen worked tirelessly to convince this farm community of the economic and environmental benefits of renewable energy. The Danish government was ready to fully invest to transform Samsø, but the locals resisted. What it took was to invite the farmers to be owners. As one observer said, "By owning the turbines themselves, people didn't feel as if the technology was imposed on them, but that they were making a smart business choice."

Looking out into Copenhagen harbor, one can't miss the wind turbines of another citizen-as-owner collaboration in Denmark: the Middlegrunden Wind Turbine Cooperative. Ownership of those turbines splits 50/50 between the municipal utility and 10,000 ordinary citizens who purchased shares in the project. Denmark is on track to get at least half of its electricity needs from wind by 2020.

Embrace Complex Collaborations

It's one thing to partner to raise money and build things, it's quite another to collaborate to change people's behavior. In this case, a city must be willing to involve a broader, more complex array of actors. Consider the case of Brownsville, Texas. Several years ago, a University of Texas School of Public Health study found that 80% of the residents of Brownsville were either obese or overweight, one in three were diabetic (50% unknowingly), and 70% of residents had no healthcare coverage. Brownsville was a very unhealthy city. The UT School of Public Health encouraged the city to establish a Community Advisory Board to oversee the changes that needed to occur. It recommended that the Advisory Board include representatives from all relevant sectors: city departments, business, academic, non-profits, health professionals, schools, and citizen groups. The city agreed and what followed was a creative and complex collaboration that transformed Brownsville.

The Brownsville City Health and Parks departments worked with a local community health clinic to launch a weekly Brownsville Farmers' Market, building community gardens on city park property to make fresh fruits and vegetables accessible and affordable to every income level in the city. The non-profit sector provides the volunteer and organizational energy that allows the farmers' market and community gardens to stay

5-29

alive. To launch a weight loss initiative, the city recruited area businesses, including the seven largest employers, to sponsor "The Challenge" as an annual event for their employees. City planning and traffic agencies, with input from citizen groups, worked on the city environment, improving signage and pathways for pedestrians and cyclists. The Community Advisory Board worked with schools to launch a play streets program and a Bikes for Tykes program, as well as stage a community health fair (5-29). The Community Advisory Board also convinced the city to pass a smoking ban ordinance. It worked with local non-profits to develop a Master Bike and Hike Plan aimed at providing a trail within one half mile of every residence in the city. Hospitals, local clinics, and practitioners participated in initiatives to increase access to health care. The Community Advisory Board, which today includes over 200 members and is a poster child for multi-dimensional, cross-sector collaborations, has ensured that Brownsville is now a much healthier place.

Involve Non-Profit Organizations

For any cross-sector collaboration, non-profit organizations should play an important role. Even for large development projects they can provide critical input regarding community needs and concerns. Non-profits often advocate for groups that are not typically involved in city projects, such as the elderly, low income residents, children, homeless, or other marginalized groups. They also can advocate for certain perspectives, such as the need for affordable housing, pedestrian safety, or environmental concerns. For some types of projects, non-profits can be a rich source of volunteers or offer outreach, event planning, or educational skills.

The Green Seattle Partnership is a good example. In 1994 the City of Seattle and the Parks Department noticed something wrong with trees in city parks. Research found that Seattle's 2,500 acres of forested city parks were at risk primarily from invasive plants such as English Ivy, but also

5-30

from trash dumping and a lack of maintenance. Local scientists predicted that about 70% of Seattle's forested parkland trees would be dead by 2025. In the past, individuals, community groups, and the city had worked independently and haphazardly to remove invasive species and conduct clean ups without knowledge of each other's activities. The problem didn't go away. To save the parks, it became clear that a cross-sector collaboration was necessary. In 2004, with the city's support, a non-profit called Green Seattle Partnership formed with the aim of arming citizens to help the city's trees. In partnership with the Department of Parks, Green Seattle Partnership is now the largest and most successful urban forest restoration project in the country, involving key city departments, over 150 businesses, local universities, environmental groups, schools, and hundreds of volunteers participating in programs, conducting research, and sponsoring events such as the annual Green Seattle Day tree planting (5-30). Today, Seattle is on track to restore all 2,500 acres of its forested parklands by 2025 *and* oversee their long-term maintenance for benefit of all who live here.

Partner with Universities

The academic sector is an important partner in efforts to make cities more sustainable and livable. Universities contribute through their mission of research, service, and through innovative teaching approaches, such as community-engaged learning.

CommUniverCity San Jose is a cross-sector partnership formed by San Jose University, the City of San Jose, and the San Jose District Community Leadership Council. This on-going collaboration—now close to 15 years old—tackles three areas for improvement in San Jose communities: neighborhood revitalization, community health, and science and technology. Each year, the organization targets a community in the San Jose area, with a focus on low-income neighborhoods. The community prioritizes its needs. Then CommUniverCity San Jose seeks faculty to add a community-engaged learning component to their classes to help address those issues. Each year a remarkable number of projects (close to 50) engage departments and classrooms across the campus. In one project, CommUniverCity San Jose tackled the problem of abandoned fruit trees along city streets. When unharvested fruit drops from city trees it attracts rodents. The collaborative project came up with a community structure for tending the trees, picking the fruit, and delivering it to food pantries and to others in need. In subsequent semesters, the project expanded to include a neighborhood gardens program (5-31), cooking classes for kids, and community education about nutritious food options.

Other universities participate in similar university-city-community collaborations. In the Pacific Northwest, the University of Oregon organizes the Sustainable Year Program; Western Washington University offers the Sustainable Communities Partnership; and the University of Washington sponsors the Livable City Year initiative. In all three cases, area cities apply to partner with the university for one year. As part of their application, city governments provide a list of challenges or opportunities facing the city. This might range from revitalizing main street to the re-design of a stormwater system. Faculty align courses with an item on the list and have students tackle the problem, presenting their results to the city at the end of the quarter, semester, or year.

5-31

Recognize Artists as Change Agents

It should be apparent throughout this book the unique and important role that artists can play in improving our cities. Artists as communicators contribute much to the mission of inviting, inspiring, and connecting people. Their talents can urge us to think about topics such as the environment, equity, and culture.

One unique type of collaboration is between scientists and artists. The mission of the Cape Farewell Project in the United Kingdom is to change the way people think about climate change. The Cape Farewell project sends scientists and artists on joint expeditions as far ranging as the Arctic and the Andes to observe first-hand, environmental change and to inspire them to become educators and activists. For climate scientists, marine biologists, botanists, geologists, artists, and communicators in all media these are transformative educational experiences. The outcomes of this creative collaboration take the form of not just published research by the scientists, but finds a voice as art installations, films, articles, performance, and

5-32

5-33

poetry. Here a Cape Farewell participant and performance artist delivers a message about the lack of trees to provide oxygen in cities (5-32).

In Minneapolis, the city government took the innovative step of embedding local artists into five different city departments to encourage creative collaborations between city departments and highly skilled artists. Funded in part by the National Endowment of the Arts, the city hopes that this three-year initiative, called Creative City-Making, will spur new approaches for interacting with the public on projects and issues facing the city. One team of artists came up with this fun Roving Green Line sidewalk train to collect local opinions about a proposed light rail extension to this neighborhood (5-33).

The barriers surrounding construction sites are temporary and often ugly. In 2015, the City of Toronto enacted legislation that requires construction

5-34

5-35

fencing (AKA hoarding) that encroaches on public space to display art. The non-profit organization PATCH acts as a curator, project manager, matchmaker, and primary liaison between artists and developers. PATCH (Public Art Through Construction Hoarding) might reproduce the work of a local artist; commission a new work specifically for the space; or engage the residents to work with an artist to produce a neighborhood-themed mural. Here, local artist Monica Wickeler created a mural called "City of Color" at a construction site for a new housing development. It features some Toronto landmarks and tells a story about community building and pride (5-34)

Artists also collaborate directly with the communities. The Neighborhood Postcard Project was an idea started by artist Hunter Franks while working with youth in the Bayview neighborhood of San Francisco. He asked the kids what they wanted to improve about their neighborhood – and there were many problems there. But the response to what they wanted to change most was, "other people's impression of Bayview." The area had a negative reputation, and residents didn't like that people looked down on them just for where they lived. This inspired Franks to work with the community to create The Postcard Project. Residents in Bayview wrote about their neighborhood on postcards, which Franks sent to random people throughout San Francisco in the hopes of breaking down stereotypes and building new community connections. This artist-community collaboration has since spread to other neighborhoods and cities. Here a girl fills out a postcard describing the best things about her San Francisco neighborhood, the Tenderloin (5-35).

Don't Forget the Kids
Former Bristol mayor George Ferguson doesn't hesitate to reveal his secret weapon for change: kids. His argument is simple. Kids are more open to change than adults. They are eager to learn about new things, whether about recycling, nutrition, or the importance of city trees. They influence their parents … and will grow up to be the next generation of community and city leaders. While mayor, Ferguson launched numerous programs that collaborated directly with kids. Perhaps the most innovative is his One Tree per Child program where *every* primary school child in the city plants a tree. Schools organize outings to plant its children's trees in places

designated by the city (5-36). This not only beautifies and improves the health of the city, but each child can watch her or his tree grow over time.

So, the message once again is: educate, engage, and collaborate. Cities need people to understand the challenges faced and act on them in positive ways. By going to where people are—using tests, events, and well-placed and timed messaging—citizens will become more informed and, ideally, more open to change. Knowing what motivates people to get involved reaps tremendous benefits in volunteer energy and the building of community. Finally, when cities collaborate across diverse sectors and actors, whether businesses, schools, artists, nonprofits, or kids, it stimulates an environment for fresh ideas and for change to happen.

5-36

6/

Moving People

Cities throughout the world are grappling with too many cars producing too many ill effects: traffic jams, lost time, frustration, expense, noise, pollution, respiratory diseases, increased greenhouse gasses and more. Another huge impact rarely considered is the amount of physical space cars take up in cities to drive and park – particularly when transporting just one person. This photo shoot organized by i-SUSTAIN, a sustainable development consulting firm, shows 2nd Avenue in downtown Seattle with 180 people in 200 cars. This number represents the known average number of people per car in this city at the time (6-1). The second photo shows the same street with the same 180 people sitting in the same spatial configuration as they would be in the cars, but without the cars. This photo makes it easy to see just how much space the car takes up to transport the people (6-2). The third photo is the same number of people in the space of one light rail car (6-3). The message here is that when city transportation departments reframe their role from one of moving vehicles to moving people, options increase. This is an important shift because most cities cannot create more streets.

In much of the United States cities grew up around the automobile. Metropolitan areas with room to spread were a welcome relief from older, industrialized cities that had become dirty and congested. A car meant freedom. The workplace no longer needed to be near home. With lots of

6-1

6-2

6-3

roads and little traffic, cars covered great distances quickly. They were big, gas was cheap, and Rachel Carson hadn't written *Silent Spring* yet.

With the oil embargo of 1973–1974, Americans got a taste of what would happen if the gush of gasoline slowed to a trickle. In subsequent years, the availability and price of gas has been relatively stable, but the problems associated with the automobile continue to erode the health and livability of cities. According to Earth Policy Institute, "In London today, the average speed of a car is about the same as that of a horse-drawn carriage from a century ago." This has psycho-social ramifications in increased stress, and when taken to the extreme, road rage. For many city dwellers, the car, once that icon of freedom and prosperity, is now an expensive and necessary evil. Car related expenses add up to be the second largest expenditure for a household next to housing.

The promising news is that reducing car use brings significant benefits to a city and its inhabitants. When options such as walking, biking, and public transit replace or complement single-occupancy vehicle trips, streets (precious publicly owned land) can fulfill more functions. In fact, this book is full of examples of using streets for diverse purposes, such as for natural stormwater infrastructure, play spaces for children, or outside seating for restaurants. Less reliance on personal cars also reduces transportation-related costs. For people who must drive, such as those who transport goods, it reduces the amount of congestion they must contend with. For those who get out of their cars, less driving decreases stress and health problems by promoting exercise and lessening traffic noise. Taking public transit can also offer personal time for reading, working, or socializing. If teenagers can get around without needing a car, everyone benefits. Up to age 35, injuries sustained through accidents involving motor vehicles are the leading cause of death. Finally, fewer cars reap significant environmental benefits.

Create Multimodal Systems

Cities need to do more than reduce traffic congestion. They need to design connected, high quality, healthy, and flexible systems for moving people. In multimodal transportation systems, cars, public transit, on-demand vehicles, bikes, walking, ferries, boats, and even gondolas become viable, affordable, and attractive options integrated in ways that streamline travel and offer convenience for the traveler. Going multimodal also fosters a more inclusive and equitable system, providing options to those who might be unable to drive due to factors such as age, health, or income.

The multimodal transportation trend is gaining traction thanks to millennials who have shown they prefer *options* and *flexibility* rather than being dependent on car ownership. Several national studies confirm that, in a given week, nearly 70% of millennials use multiple ways of getting around a city or suburb. Millennials attribute their behaviors to a desire to save money, add convenience, exercise, protect the environment, feel part of a community, and have more time for social media (while on a bus, for example). In the U.S., the percentage of youth obtaining driver's licenses has dropped significantly.

Strive for Connectivity, Convenience, and Quality

There are many features that go into creating an effective multimodal system. The first is *convenient access*. It should be easy to bike, walk, or car share to or from public transit using multi-use paths or well-located drop off areas for vehicles. At the points of connection where a traveler moves from one mode to another, the experience should be an *easy and efficient transition*. Travel payment cards should work seamlessly across all transit modes. Transit stations should have safe storage for bikes. Transit vehicles (and ideally car share vehicles) should have the capacity to carry bikes.

Moving around the city needs to be *appealing, safe, and comfortable*. Transit stops need benches, lighting, and shelters. Transit vehicles and facilities should be clean and safe, offering wireless and mobile access, as well as charging stations, and other amenities. Routes for pedestrian travel should also be appealing, with road crossings safe and easy to navigate. The same is true for biking as a mobility option with an emphasis on protected or dedicated bike paths.

The system should *function as a network*. For biking, it's particularly important that bikeways connect to allow travel across a city. The network of mobility options should also provide *accurate, real-time information* on dynamic signage and via smartphones for all points of connection. At transit stops accurate arrival and departure times enhance the quality of the travel experience. Passengers can relax or grab a cup of coffee when they know exactly when the bus is coming rather than when it is supposed to come.

While the features of a multimodal transportation system seem straightforward, designing one in a car-dominated city is challenging. For example, with more options for getting around, a person might choose to drive one day when they are late to work, ride their bike to work the next day when the weather is nice, and car-share the third day when their spouse needs the family car. How does the city plan for this? Also, a common misconception is that less reliance on personal cars equates to less people on the streets, but this is not true. Multimodal systems mean more bikes, pedestrians, taxis, car shares, and types of public transit. It becomes a puzzle to fit the moving parts together.

Supporting integrated modes of travel requires the involvement of multiple actors. Because the investment is significant, public-private partnerships can play a key role. This is happening with bike and ride-sharing services, as well as private companies providing commuter shuttles for their workers. But this also raises challenges for cities in terms of safety and oversight. For example, should private commuter shuttles use city bus stops? Where can ride-share services safely drop off passengers?

Perhaps the biggest challenge to achieving multimodal transportation systems is simply changing attitudes. It begins by dismantling the false narratives that pit car drivers against cyclists, cars against public transit, or that streets are foremost for private vehicle use. This shift in thinking is tough to achieve when alternative modes of travel are not yet in place. Street space is competitive. When cities reassign vehicle travel or parking lanes to bicycle paths without good alternatives people get understandably frustrated. Ideally, public transit options are in place prior to reducing lanes for cars. We've seen this in some European cities, resulting in a less traumatic transition. In U.S. cities, this approach rarely happens.

Prioritize the Pedestrian Experience

Walkable streets might be one of the best indicators of a livable and sustainable city. The tremendous benefits to a city of prioritizing the pedestrian experience make for a compelling and long list. Here's just a sampler. When people choose to walk they make their neighborhoods safer and more vibrant. Walkable neighborhoods increase opportunities for social interaction and the building of community. Regular walkers enjoy better health and live longer. Choosing to walk instead of drive is better for the environment by reducing air pollution and traffic noise, and decreasing reliance

6-4

on oil. Walking promotes local culture and sense of place as pedestrian-friendly cities tend to have more public art, events, and activities in public spaces. Pedestrian-friendly streets encourage public transit use because people are more likely to walk to transit stops. Walkable cities are more inclusive and equitable; it's a mode of travel everyone can afford and most can do.

There are financial benefits as well. Businesses located in areas frequented by pedestrians often see retail sales go up. Walkable areas tend to attract more private investment and tourists. According to a University of Washington study, in King County, pedestrian friendly, compact neighborhoods have a positive impact on property values. This is a benefit for homeowners, real estate developers, and city services that rely on property taxes, though issues with gentrification can arise.

Finally, walking is great for kids. According to the U.S. Centers for Disease Control and Prevention (CDC) obesity has nearly doubled in children and quadrupled in adolescents in the past 30 years. Childhood obesity has many negative effects, including high cholesterol, cardiovascular disease, high blood pressure, bone and joint problems, sleep apnea, poor self-esteem and victimization from bullying. To promote children's health, neighbors across the world are organizing "walking school busses." The concept is simple. As shown here, local children walk to and from school together (in their "make-believe" school bus) with one or more adults (6-4). This provides daily exercise and builds community as neighbors get to know each other.

Plan for Connectivity

"Pick Your Winners," writes Jeff Speck in his book *Walkable City* to make the point that not every street in a city will be walkable. Instead, he argues, cities should identify walkable areas and within them create networks of appealing and natural pathways that connect people to where they want and need to go. Too many outdoor pedestrian "malls" in the United States failed when they provided access to shopping and restaurants only, emulating indoor shopping malls. By contrast, the inherent connectivity of mixed-use areas promotes walking by offering a range of services, from groceries to health care to hardware stores. Pedestrian friendly areas have frequent street connections and pathways to easily get to amenities with few barriers, such as difficult-to-cross streets.

6-5

Moving People

Let Pedestrians Rule

Changing the status of a street to pedestrian only or pedestrian priority takes us back to an earlier time. In fact, the older parts of a city—with narrow streets created before motorized vehicle use—lend themselves well to pedestrian only or pedestrian priority status. What people notice most is the relaxed feel of these streets compared with the surrounding vehicle-dominated streets. Throughout the world, people flock to pedestrian only streets for shopping, dining, and socializing. Pedestrian priority streets allow pedestrians and vehicles to co-exist, but the vehicles must slow to the walkers' pace as shown on this shared use street in Istanbul (6-5).

The Downtown Mall in Charlottesville, Virginia began as a colonial route in the 1730s, a route that three early U.S. presidents—Thomas Jefferson, James Madison, and James Monroe—undoubtedly walked on when they lived in the area. Lost to cars, then reclaimed in the 1970s, it is now one of the longest and most successful pedestrian streets in the United States with a great mix of shops and restaurants housed in historic buildings. It is the place to dine, listen to music, and to see and be seen (6-6).

6-6

6-7   6-8

In its rush to modernization, Shanghai like many Chinese cities tore down much of its historical architecture. A welcome exception is the maze of narrow lanes in the French Concession, Tianzifang, where circa 1930s buildings include 20 distinct styles of Shikumen "Stone Warehouse Gate" houses and small former factories. The Shikumen-style dates to 1869 and represents both eastern and western architectural styles. Shops and residences line the narrow alleys of Tianzifang with their high brick walls and unique stone-framed doors that historically provided access to the private yards. Local artist Chen Yifei helped save the area from razing and new development to see it reinvented as a popular, comparatively quiet part of the city for eating, shopping, and imagining what 1930s Shanghai might have been like (6-7). Unfortunately, this narrow street with beautiful carved doors, also in Shanghai, was torn down without an eye to preservation (6-8).

Attract Pedestrians to the Downtown Core

In 2007 Mexico City, one of the largest cities in the world, initiated a comprehensive revitalization program—Plan Verde—to make the city more sustainable. To tackle the city's dangerous levels of smog, the city government is working hard to reduce vehicle use by boosting mass transit and bicycle infrastructure and pedestrianizing several major streets in the historic center, Centro Histórico. The challenge of reclaiming streets such as Calle Regina and Calle Francisco I. Madero included not just re-routing

6-9   6-10

traffic, but clearing out gang influences and convincing business owners from other parts of the city to relocate their businesses there. A public-private partnership between the government of Mexico City and a Mexican telecom billionaire spent large sums to rehabilitate historic buildings, make infrastructure improvements, and increase security. Today, the once deteriorated, crime-ridden heart of the city is a vibrant, pedestrian-friendly neighborhood of shops, restaurants, galleries, and museums (6-9).

Jerusalem is known for many things: the spiritual home of the three great monotheistic religions, the historical battleground between Christians and Muslims, the controversial capital of modern-day Israel, and the desired capital of the Palestinians. In the mix are sporadic episodes of horrific violence by suicide bombers. Located in the heart of downtown Jerusalem, a city known for its intensity, the cobblestoned pedestrian mall of Ben Yehuda Street is a relaxing refuge (6-10). Instead of traffic and honking horns, one hears the murmur of many languages as people shop for fine art or tee shirts, eat at expensive restaurants or shawarma stands, enjoy street musicians, or people watch.

In Melbourne, Australia changing the pedestrian experience revitalized that city's downtown, once a described as a donut – empty in the center. In 1992 a portion of the heavily travelled Swanston Street—the city's main north-south thoroughfare—became a pedestrian and tram street with access only for small delivery and emergency vehicles. The city improved Swanston and other major streets for pedestrians through the widening of sidewalks to almost 30 feet on each side, adding attractive street furniture and greenery, encouraging outdoor cafes, and changing codes to make the first floor of buildings more visually interesting to pedestrians. As a result, pedestrian traffic increased by almost 40% during the day and 98% at night. By 2010, the city decided to make the entire length of Swanston Street car-free, adding more public squares and tram stops.

Protect People

Many factors encourage people to walk, including frequency and ease of street connections, amenities, and services, sidewalk availability and quality, and aesthetics. The chapter on Inviting People describes many ways to enhance street appeal in cities. One of the most important factors mentioned, and emphasized again here, is safety. People will not walk if they do not feel safe, and with good reason. According to the Governors Highway Safety Association's 2017 report, U.S. pedestrian deaths increased to their highest level in over 20 years, in part due to ubiquitous smartphone use that distracts both drivers and pedestrians. Cities and states are implementing fines and educational campaigns to get drivers to refrain from phone use while driving, but pedestrians also need to be aware of their surroundings.

Making streets feel safe for walking includes slowing vehicles through both street design and speed limits of 20 mph or less, signaled crosswalks with countdown timers, pedestrian islands for broad boulevards, well maintained sidewalks that separate walkers from drivers (unless a pedestrian priority street), good street lighting at night, warning signs (6-11),

6-11

6-12

Moving People

plenty of other people on the street, and shops and residences whose windows provide "eyes on to the street."

Also important is having relatively even surface materials, even when using bricks and cobblestone, maintaining the street surface for cracks, removing snow or slippery leaves, and insuring that there is a clear pathway without obstacles. This is particularly important for the blind, elderly or wheelchair bound. Safety and comfort are very closely related, but comfort also includes protection from the elements such as shade trees in hot climates, awnings in places where it is gets hot or rainy, a place to sit such as attractive public benches or outdoor café tables, and smaller blocks. Here, a bench in Washington, D.C. provides mobile phone charging through a solar panel (6-12).

When people visit Washington, D.C. they are often surprised by how much walking they do. This is because the District is inherently walkable, the legacy of the first urban plan by Pierre L'Enfant in 1791. According to the District Department of Transportation 12% of the District's residents walk to work, which is nearly twice the national average. In a commitment to prioritize walking and bicycling at the same level as driving, the District drafted its first Pedestrian Plan in 2009. An important contributor to the walkability of the city is that traffic light timing allows pedestrians ample time to cross the oftentimes broad boulevards without feeling hurried. This results in fewer pedestrian-vehicle collisions. Signals display exactly how much time remains to cross the street (6-13).

6-13

6-14

6-15

6-16

Moving People

Some other approaches to pedestrian safety can be found in the Brummen municipality, Netherlands where crosswalks light up (6-14). Or in Madrid, where Bulgarian artist Christo Guelov's series of crosswalk art (called *Funnycross)* is not just an attempt to brighten the day of local Madrileños, but to slow traffic and increase pedestrian safety by high-lighting crosswalks (6-15)

Some cities are even installing 3-D crosswalks. This example from a small town in Iceland creates an optical illusion so the drivers see a raised crosswalk with people seeming to float across (6-16), causing them to slow down. The local commissioner in charge of the project got her idea from another successful 3-D crossing painted in New Dehli, India.

In La Paz, Bolivia *cebritas* roam the street. The zebras are part of a city program to keep wild drivers in line and protect pedestrians. Based on a similar—and very successful—program in Bogotá in the 1990s where the city employed mimes to shame drivers who broke traffic laws, in La Paz the herd of zebras can't issue tickets but they can dance, gesture, and assist pedestrians across the street (6-17). The program started with 24 zebras in 2001. In 2017, there were 265 zebras in La Paz (plus more in other cities). Another innovative twist to the award-winning *cebritas* program is that many are students from disadvan-taged backgrounds who are given the chance to work part time as fun-loving, people-protecting zebras. One of the program organizers confirms local drivers are more careful and courteous since the zebras arrived, and that the general mood on the streets has improved.

6-17

Don't Forget the Details

In designing pedestrian infrastructure, details become important. Public stairs in Sweden frequently include ramps to use for wheelchairs, bicycles, wheeled suitcases, or baby carriages (6-18). Pedestrians and cyclists are very sensitive to weak links in an infrastructure system. If there is only one gap that is difficult to navigate, in an otherwise comprehensive network, that alone will deter many people from walking or riding their bikes.

Details such as pedestrian signals can even convey a sense of place, history, and values. Vienna, Austria boldly used some of their walk signals to convey that it is a gay friendly city (6-19). This Ampelmännchen signal is a carryover from the days of a divided Germany when East and West functioned under two separate governments and traffic signal systems (6-20). The now iconic little man with the hat, developed in East Germany, appears throughout the country on tee shirts, souvenir cups, and almost everything else that tourists might want to buy.

6-18

6-19   6-20

6-21

Walk Score **86** Transit Score **80** Bike Score **71**

6-22

Keep Track

Understanding travel patterns is essential for the wise use of limited municipal funds. Most cities have a Department of Transportation that keeps close count, for planning purposes, on how many vehicles travel its main streets and highways. Few, however, quantify cycling and walking. An exception is Arlington, Virginia, where bicycle and pedestrian counters capture round-the-clock data on street and trail use by non-motorized travel, allowing the public to see the results. In 2009, the City of Melbourne developed a 24/7 system that monitors pedestrian activity within the city center and other areas. The online visualization tool, currently comprised of 28 pedestrian counting sensors, records movements only (not images), to maintain privacy. The local government uses the data to evaluate infrastructure investments and the impact of major events, improve walking conditions, and assist with emergency response planning (6-21).

Cities are finding that people are willing to pay a premium for housing in neighborhoods that are walking distance to shops, restaurants, doctors, employment, and public transit.

Walkscore.com is a company that assigns numerical walk, transit, and bike scores to cities and neighborhoods. Here is how San Francisco scores (6-22). While some critics point out that the Walkscore formula doesn't take into consideration walk appeal (e.g., amount of greenery or the presence of sidewalks), real estate brokerages are now using these numbers when marketing a property.

Build a Bicycle Culture

To transition to an effective multimodal transportation system, cities require a well-connected bicycle infrastructure. Users should be able to reach all significant destinations, safely and efficiently, solely on their bike or in seamless combination with other modes of travel such as public transit. With little, no, or poor bicycle infrastructure cyclists are forced to travel in

6-23

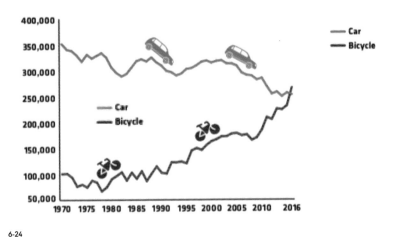

TRAFFIC CROSSING THE CITY CENTER IN COPENHAGEN 1970-2016

6-24

the same lanes as cars, accidents are all too commonplace with devastating outcomes. In conflicts between vehicles and bicycles, bicycles always lose.

Equally important is to build a bicycle culture. For example, people of every age, from school children to senior citizens, should receive training on the rules of the road for cycling. In Odense, Denmark, this bicycle class is part of the regular school curriculum (6-23). Cities also need to educate and test vehicle drivers on safety when near pedestrians and cyclists. Ironically, when the number of cyclists increase in a city, the numbers of accidents involving cyclists decrease. This is because drivers learn to look for cyclists when they switch lanes, make a turn to cross the bike path, or open their car door.

Cities throughout the world are embracing cycling as a viable means of transportation that deserves adequate funding. Fortunately, there are some good role models. Amsterdam and Copenhagen, for example, are far ahead in creating a safe and efficient bicycle environment. It is important to note, though, that although Denmark has a long history of bicycling, during the 1970s, as the graph below shows, bicycling was at an all-time low and car use was at an all-time high (6-24). At the time of the oil crisis, Denmark was 98% dependent on foreign energy. In reaction to the crisis, the country re-embraced bicycling, as well as energy efficiency and the development of sustainable and renewable energy solutions.

6-25   6-26

Lessons from Copenhagen

In Copenhagen, bicycling is part of the culture. In a city with more bikes than inhabitants, 50% of the people commute to work or school each day by bicycle. Everyone rides bikes, regardless of purpose, income level, or time of year. In fact, ridership figures decline only by about 20% during the cold and sometimes snowy winter months. A key reason for this is that the city actively maintains both the bicycling and vehicle infrastructure. Here, street cleaners keep the bike lanes free from debris with a specialized vehicle (6-25). In the winter, the city often removes snow from the cycle paths before moving to the vehicle streets (6-26).

A crucial ingredient of a successful bicycle culture is that there is a place for everyone. Pedestrians have wide sidewalks or pedestrian only or pedestrian priority streets, and bicyclists have their own very distinct lanes, with vehicles kept at a safe distance. In Copenhagen, bike lanes clearly marked with intersections crossings painted blue (6-27). Bicyclists generally follow the rules and know they must dismount their bikes on a pedestrian only street (6-28).

Bicycle lanes have robust infrastructure including their own traffic lights and signs. Most signal timing gives bicyclists a head start so they can get in front of the cars, which is much safer (6-29). In this photo, the Cycle Snake elevates bicyclists above particularly congested Copenhagen streets (6-30). Shop owners have discovered that giving up a few parking spaces for bicyclists can increase the number of patrons (6-31). In fact, bike parking is widely available throughout the city providing a boost to local businesses (6-32). Approximately 40,000 cargo bikes in use each day provide a place to put groceries, children, and all manner of objects (6-33, 6-34). Green

6-27

6-28

6-29

6-30

6-31

Waves, bicycle routes where traffic lights always give bicyclists travelling at the signed speed a green light are very popular with commuters in from the suburbs.

The Danes calculated that 3.5 pounds of carbon dioxide and nine cents in health care costs savings result from every six miles biked. In Copenhagen, annually this equates to 90,000 tons of CO2 emissions not produced. Danes get free medical care throughout their lives, paid for by taxes, so reducing health care costs is also a very important economic priority for the government and the citizens. It's worth mentioning that the people of Denmark rank as the happiest people on earth in several international surveys, including the United Nations World Happiness Report. While there are many reasons, one surely is from having a bicycle culture.

6-32

6-33

6-34

Moving People

Bike Share Programs

It just takes one look at the Bike Sharing World Map (http://www.bikesharingworld.com) to see that bike share programs are springing up rapidly around the world. The low rental cost and flexibility associated with bike share programs make them a desirable component of a multimodal transportation system both as a primary mode of travel or to fill in "first and last mile" gaps between public transit stops and someone's start or destination.

Cities from Barcelona to Hangzhou to Mexico City to Seattle and Paris are trying on different formats, sizes, and ownership approaches to see what works for their geography, demographic, and budget. The Paris system Vélib' represents a public-private partnership in which the bike share system is paid for by the French advertising agency JCDecaux. In exchange, JCDecaux gets advertising revenue. Bike share programs such as Vélib that place docking stations around the city generally require a periodic redistribution of the bikes. Cyclists, for example, may park their bikes at the bottom of a downhill commute in the morning and take the bus uphill in the evening. Redistribution brings the bikes back up the hill ready for the morning commute (6-35). The Washington, D.C. system,

6-35

6-36   6-37

6-38

Capital Bikeshare, began as a partnership between the District Department of Transportation and Clear Channel. Considered an integral part of the public transit system, it receives government support (6-36). Citibank helped finance the launch of the New York bike share system to regain public trust after the financial crisis through the promotion of sustainable cities. The intent was for the program to become self-supporting, but this is not the case (6-37). One of the largest bike share programs in the world is in Hangzhou, China. In 2008 there were 2,965 stations with 69,750 bikes. This is supposed to reach almost 200,000 bikes by 2020. The success of Hangzhou's bicycle sharing program is its integration with public transit. A

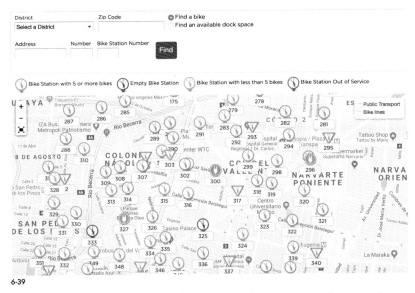

6-39

smart card provides access to all forms of public transit including subway, bus, ferry, taxi, and bike share. What is most remarkable is that this city has successfully overcome the perception that bicycling is a low status activity, which it was for many years (6-38).

In 2010, as part of Mexico City's Plan Verde (Green Plan) the government launched a bike share program, Ecobici, starting with 1,200 bikes at 90 stations and plans to grow to 4,000 bikes at 275 stations and 73,000 users. Bikes are much more efficient in Mexico City rush hour traffic. They typically travel at over six mph while cars travel at 2.5 mph.

However, the most unique commitment the city has made is to close 14 miles of downtown and near downtown streets to vehicles every Sunday, in an initiative called, "Muevete en Bici," which means Bike Move. Every Sunday, thousands of cyclists along with pedestrians, rollerbladers, skateboarders, and others enjoy the rolling party. The goal is to get citizens to enjoy biking enough to exert pressure to improve and enhance the nascent bicycling infrastructure.

Bike share riders throughout the world, including those in Mexico City, use smartphones to determine the location of nearby bike stations, see how many bikes are there, and determine which routes to take (6-39). Portland,

Oregon is developing a unique concept in which people can purchase rental bikes and use the rental income to pay for the bikes over time.

The bike share world is changing quickly. Seattle is an example of multiple private bike share companies vying for market share by providing dockless bikes, including electric bikes to get up Seattle's many hills. Dockless bike share systems allow riders to leave their bike anywhere. This is not without controversy as bikes are sometimes improperly parked blocking pedestrians and other cyclists. Scooter share systems are also popping up in many cities.

Bicycling Amenities

A good bicycling network functions at both the macro and micro levels. At the macro level, the system must be comprehensive enough to safely and efficiently get people where they want to go. In 2015, a pilot project in Calgary built a four-mile network of connected downtown bike lanes. During the 18-month trial, downtown ridership increased 40% mostly on the protected lanes. As a result, the City Council voted to make the bike lanes permanent.

People also need places to safely park their bikes. In Tokyo, a city of over 13 million, bicyclists ride a short distance from their home or work to the subway or train, then rely on the city's excellent public transportation network for the longer stretches. As a result, the city provides 2.4 million

6-40

bicycle parking spaces in stations and lots near trains and subways. Although there is a fee for bicycle parking in Tokyo, users receive many benefits. These mostly monitored lots reduce theft, and often provide pumps, maintenance tools, and shower facilities. With indoor lots the bikes stay dry when it rains. There are a variety of types of lots including large multi-level parking lots near metro stations that have storage for thousands of bikes. Upon entry, riders get a ticket from the machine, manually park their bike in the garage, and pay upon exiting (6-40). More technologically advanced

Moving People

6-41

6-42   6-43   6-44

bicycle parking lots use robotics to whisk bicycles underground for storage. The advantage is that they use a minimal amount of precious above ground space (6-41).

At the micro level, even a small gap in the network that feels unsafe or is too difficult to navigate in an otherwise excellent system will deter people from bicycling. An example of filling a gap are the bike gutters used in Copenhagen and Tokyo to help people negotiate stairs. This stairway with the bike gutter in Copenhagen leads down to the city's central train station (6-42). This bicycle gutter in Tokyo is in a large multi-level bicycle parking lot (6-43). Also in Tokyo is this bicycle escalator adjacent to a staircase emerging from Tamachi Station (6-44). Public transportation in the Puget

6-45

6-46

6-47

6-48

Sound area of Washington state accommodates bicycles (6-45 and 6-46). In a robust system, bicycling and public transit work together to provide a complete network that oftentimes is faster and less expensive than driving a car and far better for the environment and public health.

Washington, D.C. provides a great service to bicycle, train, metro, bus commuters, and tourists at Union Station, the region's largest transportation hub. The contemporary bike services structure provides indoor secure parking spaces, lockers, showers, pumps, tools and a full-service bike repair shop (6-47). Just outside of the building are private rental bikes and bike share bikes.

In the Seattle area, King County added do-it-yourself bike repair and pump stations outside of 10 branch library locations (6-48). In addition to basic tools to do common repairs, the stands also feature QR codes. A quick smartphone scan provides access to short videos for bicycle repairs.

Commit to Public Transit

Cities face a wave of population growth and change. Today, for the first time in history, over half the world's population lives in urban areas. By 2050 that figure will grow to 70%. More than ever, cities need to develop affordable public transit systems that provide local and regional services. Cities need to include a broad range of integrated services such as trains (heavy rail), light rail, subways, buses, trams, shuttles, ferries, taxis, gondolas, and car shares. To attract riders, public transit must be accessible, affordable, and equitable. It must be efficient, frequent, and reliable. Riders must feel comfortable and safe. And, it's becoming increasingly important that public transit systems offer more flexible and on-demand options for travel.

Accessible, Affordable, and Equitable

Urban and transportation planners within city governments are leading the charge for Transit-Oriented Development (TOD), in which retail businesses, offices, residences, and public transit cluster together both inside and outside the city center. This approach positions transit stops and stations as part of a pedestrian-friendly neighborhood so access is easy and comfortable. TOD isn't without its detractors. It often includes increasing height limits and bringing mixed-use buildings into traditionally single-family neighborhoods. Although people often enjoy the added amenities TOD brings such as shopping and restaurants, they don't always want it in their own neighborhood. Throughout the world cities are grappling with how to have more TOD, and the population density that comes with it, while still maintaining the existing character of a neighborhood.

Whatever the development strategy, the benefits are many. A good public transit system saves riders money. According to a 2013 AAA study, the average cost of owning and operating a car is 60.8 cents per mile, or $9,122 per year, based upon 15,000 miles of annual driving. According to the Federal Highway Administration, households that are auto-dependent, spend 25% of their income on transportation costs. Households living closer to work spend just 9%. When a city has a reliable and efficient transit system supplemented by ride-sharing, people can do without cars entirely or use them more sparingly. Not having car payments, maintenance costs, and fuel costs can mean more money in the bank, a closer-in neighborhood or nicer home, and more vacations.

Not everyone can afford to live in the city center. The gondola in Medellín, Metrocable, is not only a public transit solution, but a social justice solution. Medellín's public transit system did not serve the populated, but underdeveloped sections of the city. Neither the regular bus system nor Medellín's Metro could reach the steep neighborhoods, which meant that it took many workers up to five hours to commute to and from work each week. Started in 2004, the gondola fully integrates into the Metro system (6-49).

Efficient, Frequent, and Reliable

To attract riders, efficiency, frequency, and reliability of service are most important. Ideally, the bus, tram, subway, or light rail should come by so often that schedules are unnecessary. People should know that whenever they show up, the wait time will only be a few minutes. When waits are longer, arrival times should be available on real-time GPS-driven electronic displays at the stops or stations and on smartphone apps. When on the bus, electronic feeds should display the next stop. Traffic signal priority for public transit, in which the bus or streetcar always has a green light, increases the efficiency of public transit over other vehicles and encourages car drivers to ride the bus when they see it passing them.

When done well, Bus Rapid Transit or BRT embodies all these things. It is the least expensive and most efficient method of transporting masses of people along a fixed route. It functions much like an above ground subway on rubber tires using dedicated surface street lanes. Fares are collected prior to boarding, and the height of the platform is at the same level as the bus for quick loading and unloading which works well for the disabled or those with strollers or wheelchairs. When the doors open, the passengers pour out of multiple exits and new riders board just like a subway. Total stop time is typically less than 20 seconds (6-50). Busses run frequently, oftentimes just a couple of minutes apart. BRT is appearing in cities throughout the world although some cities "cheat" and only use some aspects of the system, which they then inappropriately refer to it as BRT. A true BRT system must have dedicated bus lanes.

6-49

6-50

6-51

6-52

The development of BRT in Curitiba was part of a larger Transit-Oriented Development (TOD) land use strategy adopted in a master plan from the 1960s. Rather than let the city center sprawl haphazardly into the surrounding areas, transit corridors radiated out from the city center and served as spines around which dense industrial, commercial, and residential development grew. Zoning provided for greater building heights closer to the corridors and decreasing building heights farther away from the corridors. The tall buildings next to the BRT corridors serve to protect the smaller scale residential neighborhoods behind them from pollution and noise (6-51).

6-53   6-54

A variation of Bus Rapid Transit is Tram Rapid Transit (TRT) in Istanbul. Just like BRT, the passengers prepay and are pre-staged. Trams have their own dedicated space and do not have to compete with cars (6-52).

In fact, trams are making a comeback throughout the world. Trams are less polluting and quieter than bus travel. While traditional trams tended to attach to overhead electric wires, the modern generation of trams use a third rail embedded in the ground to provide electricity. A few cities, like Melbourne, never dismantled their tram systems, but instead chose to upgrade. Today Melbourne boasts the largest tram system in the world covering 150 miles of double tracks, 29 routes, and 1,763 stops to attract almost 200 million passengers boarding each year. The tram system is an integral part of Melbourne's identity (6-53) with historic trams still used on the touristy Circle Line (6-54) and tram images showing up on a myriad of souvenirs.

Comfort and Safety

A great public transit system is a well-used public transit system. Safety is essential to getting people to use public transit. People must feel secure while waiting for the bus or train, particularly at night when the stations and stops should be well lit, clean, and protected from the weather. Operators should protect passengers from harassment or personal discomfort.

Safe public transit systems also free up precious time for families. Rather than having parents chauffeuring their children, children can take public transit themselves. Evidence also suggests that people who use public transit walk more than those who drive and, therefore, are in

6-55   6-56

better health. A greater reliance on public transit increases air quality and decreases traffic-related injuries.

Flexible and On-Demand

Flexibility is an attractive feature as part of a public transit system. Here is where smaller vehicles or on-demand services like taxis or car shares can play integral roles in a public transit system.

Colectivos in San Cristóbal de las Casas and other cities in Mexico provide an invaluable service for passengers and an income for entrepreneurs. Privately operated, colectivos park at designated areas based on destination. The vehicle itself states where it is going. When there are enough passengers, the colectivo leaves for the stated destination (6-55). Colectivos are just as important in rural areas where in small villages and along roadways people flag them down. Some large companies in cities like San Francisco and Seattle use the colectivo concept, transporting employees on private vans or buses when the city transit systems are inadequate, although this practice is not without controversy.

Water taxis are a nice way of getting people around a city using urban waterways. The Victoria, BC water taxi functions just like a regular taxi. It picks up passengers on an as needed basis, and passengers pay the water taxi captain directly (6-56).

Cities are also figuring out the best ways to integrate a variety of new micro-transit options including on-demand car, ride, and bike share companies, electric vehicles, and driverless cars. These options not only add flexibility to a city's mobility system, but can fill the gaps by reaching underserved areas or reducing the need for parking at transit stations. For micro-transit options, cities often look to private-public partnerships. For example, in Dublin, California the local transit authority is working with both Lyft and Uber to subsidize van pool rides to reduce congestion and the need for parking space at the city's rail station. In Los Angeles, the city is looking for partners to develop its own micro-transit system, using on-demand mini-buses. In King County, Washington, a private-public partnership offers Trailhead Direct, a program that shuttles hikers and mountain bikers to and from different area trailheads, leaving every 30 minutes on weekends and holidays, to enjoy the outdoors without worrying about a car (6-57).

For any multimodal transportation system to be effective, cities must turn to technology for comprehensive management of that system to facilitate flow and safety and to place less stress on the environment. Integration and cohesiveness will be keys to success because, if there is one thing we know, it's that the roads of our future will not be less busy, they will be different. People will increasingly move through cities drawing on a broader transportation portfolio. In cities around the world expect to see roadways increasingly modified to host multiple uses and users, whether personal vehicles, transit, pedestrians, bikes, or other forms yet to emerge.

6-57

7/

Supporting People

Today's cities must provide people with many basics for our safety and survival, including clean water, access to healthy food and medical care, shelter, and energy. Because each of these categories is so vital and encompasses so many different aspects of urban life, it is not possible to cover them in a comprehensive way in this book. Instead, this chapter focuses on some intriguing ideas related to food, energy, and water that share a common theme: the role of nature as a source for food and energy; as a promoter of health; and as a design partner in the management of energy, climate, and water.

Increase Food Quality and Security

Food security and sustainability is a global issue. The United Nations predicts that the world will need to increase its food production 70% by 2050 to feed a population predicted to rise from seven to nine billion. At the same time, current agricultural practices are not sustainable. They are destroying forests, habitats, and biodiversity worldwide. What can cities do? They can help bring food closer to home. Food production and distribution, for years the purview of agribiz in rural areas and major grocery chains in urban areas, is changing as people realize the benefits of eating local.

Urban Farming

Support of urban farming is a critical way that cities can support people. Cities can encourage people to grow their own food in several ways, including the permanent or temporary provision of land, plants, materials, and training, as well as updating policies and zoning codes. For example, Seattle passed an ordinance that allows homeowners to plant vegetable gardens in their parking strips which are not private property, but part of the street right-of-way.

There are many reasons why urban dwellers of every economic level have taken to growing their own food. Some find that gardening and cooking with ingredients they have grown is pleasurable. Others do it to supplement their income. While still others grow food out of necessity. The reason often dictates the scale at which it happens.

Vivero Alamar is an example of a large-scale urban farm that arose out of necessity. Located in the Alamar neighborhood, a suburb of Havana, it is one of Cuba's most successful neighborhood-managed cooperative organic farms (7-1). The farm emerged after the fall of the Soviet Union when significant food imports (which accounted for 57% of Cuban's caloric intake) and subsidized fuel used to transport food from the countryside disappeared. Cuba suddenly needed to feed itself. Confronting an alarming food shortage, the 2.2 million citizens of Havana began planting bananas, tomatoes, beans on balconies and terraces, in empty lots and backyards. Vivero Alamar began in 1997 on nine acres of what founder Miguel

7-1

7-2

Salcines refers to as abandoned wasteland surrounded by Soviet-style apartment buildings. Today the farm sells 90% of its 300 tons and 27 acres of produce directly to the public. The rest sells at reduced prices to schools and hospitals. Over 160 people work at Vivero Alamar, one of the largest organopónicos (organic farms) in Cuba.

Vivero Alamar and the other Cuban farms became organic by necessity since there weren't any petroleum-based fertilizer and pesticides coming in from the Soviet Union anymore. Fortunately, the farms remain organic. Employees collectively own most organopónicos, sharing the profits. Compared with other industries, these workers do very well and are an important part of the food system. Data from 2011 states that 87,000 acres of land in and around the perimeters of Havana is devoted to urban agriculture and accounts for 60% to 90% of the produce consumed in the city.

Also born out of necessity, though not as dire as the situation in Cuba, Seattle's P-Patch Community Gardens started as the brainstorm of a University of Washington student, Darlyn Rundberg del Boca, in the early 1970s as a creative solution to sudden economic hardship. Aerospace employment in the region dropped from 98,000 at the end of 1968 to 29,000 by mid-1971 due to the cancellation of Boeing's supersonic transport (SST) program. At the time, Seattle was a one company town, and this catastrophe resulted in unemployment jumping from 2.9 to 13.1%. A famous Seattle billboard implored, "Would the last person leaving Seattle turn out the lights?" This was a difficult period for previously well-paid workers and their families who now needed assistance with necessities like food. Ms. Ruberg del Boca created a community vegetable garden for children at the site of a local truck farm owned by the Picardo family. Soon after, she got permission to expand the project to include 8' x 8' plots of garden space for families in need. The food from the first garden was donated to Neighbors in Need, the precursor to Washington State's hunger relief organization, Northwest Harvest. The original Picardo Family community garden is still part of Seattle's P-Patch network (the family's founding role accounts for the "P" in P-Patch) with 259 plots of 100 to 800 sq. ft. (7-2). Today there are over 80 P-Patch community gardens throughout the city, including a large one in downtown Seattle. The City of Seattle Department of Neighborhoods now manages the program.

Aside from providing a local source of healthy organic produce,

Supporting People

community gardens show how a good idea can provide multiple benefits. Community gardens foster community and social interaction, assist immigrants used to growing their own food adjust to their new life, provide a peaceful respite from city noise and congestion, provide outdoor space for apartment dwellers, help keep the residents, particularly the elderly, active, reduce neighborhood blight, and improve air quality. Many community gardens now found across the United States continue the tradition of Seattle's P-Patches to teach children about gardening and provide food for distribution to those in need. In 2012, P-Patch gardeners donated almost 30,000 pounds of fresh organic produce to Seattle area food banks. Another reason for urban gardens is resiliency during a crisis. Victory Gardens were important to the well-being of cities during WWII.

High Point Juneau Community Garden in West Seattle participates in the Seattle P-Patch Market Gardens program. The mission of the Market Gardens program is "to help establish safe, healthy communities and economic opportunity through development of CSA and farm stand enterprises in low-income neighborhoods." Gardeners living in the Highpoint housing development can sell the food they produce thus creating an additional source of income. CSA or Community Supported Agriculture refers to a partnership between farmers and consumers who receive weekly deliveries of produce throughout the growing season, for a set price.

Another type of urban farming is SPIN farming. SPIN stands for Small Plot Intensive, a type of agriculture in which urban farmers contract with homeowners, typically within the same neighborhood for logistical reasons, to turn under-used residential yards into sub-acre plots for intensive crop production. In exchange for providing the land and water, homeowners get fresh produce and a beautiful garden without having to do any of the work. SPIN farmers, who sell the produce at premium prices at local farmers' markets and through CSAs, find that the urban environment provides a better growing environment than rural areas because growing seasons are longer, there are less insects and other pests and, frequently, less wind. However, the biggest benefit for SPIN farmers is that the use of the land is free or very inexpensive. Typically, the biggest cost for near-city farmers is the land cost. Also, with SPIN farming located within cities, transportation costs and time to market are greatly reduced.

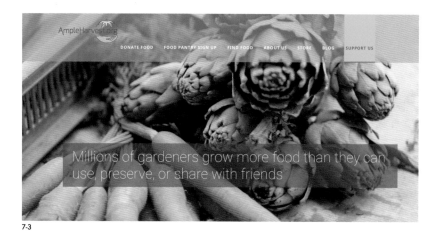

Millions of gardeners grow more food than they can use, preserve, or share with friends

7-3

Add a little technology to backyard food growing and more people in need get fresh, nutritious and delicious food. A self-described aging geek with a background in computers and communication, Gary Oppenheimer, created the non-profit AmpleHarvest.org (7-3). His involvement with a community garden in 2009 inspired his idea to use the Internet to connect people with excess produce to food pantries and other local food distribution facilities that could distribute it to those in need. According to the National Gardening Association, people throw an estimated $100 billion worth of food away annually in the U.S. of which over 40 million pounds is from backyard gardeners who produce more than they can consume, preserve, or give away. One out of every six Americans, or 50 million people, rely on food assistance but local food distribution centers often don't have access to fresh produce. The implementation of the AmpleHarvest.org idea is elegantly simple. AmpleHarvest.org provides the location and driving instructions to about 7,000 food distribution facilities, often called food pantries, in 50 states. It lists desired days and times for receiving donations, as well as what items specific facilities are hoping to get.

Another innovative food distribution solution, targeting those in need, comes from Curitiba, Brazil. Years of rapid population growth resulted in a perimeter belt of city slums and informal neighborhoods called favelas. Without money or road access for sanitation trucks people routinely disposed of garbage in open water and fields, resulting in serious health

Supporting People

7-4   7-5

and environmental problems. As a creative solution, the city instituted a program called "Garbage that is not Garbage," or "O Lixo que Não é Lixo" in Portuguese, that encouraged all Curitibans to separate recyclable materials from organic waste. The program provided new jobs for the urban poor as cart-pushers and sorters. A complementary organization, "Green Exchange" (Cambio Verde) started two years later. As part of this program, two trucks come to the edge of the favelas; one truck to collect recyclables and the other full of nutritious food to distribute to the residents in exchange for their recyclables based on weight (7-4, 7-5). If residents receive more food than they need they can make extra income by selling it. In addition to food, the city sometimes distributes bus tickets, and even movie tickets.

Another aspect of this program is that the food distributed as part of the Green Exchange comes from "Solidarity Farm," a 200-acre farm that provides drug and alcohol treatment for men. The men work the fields and learn carpentry, baking and other trades. The success of these programs is apparent as the favelas, and much of the rest of the city, are virtually waste free with residents' diet much improved. Eventually, more than 70% of households in Curitiba became involved in these innovative programs, contributing to this southern Brazilian city earning the title of the "Ecological Capital" of Brazil. A school-based version of the program supplies under-resourced students with schoolbooks and toys at Christmas.

A food forest employs permaculture – a gardening technique or land management system that mimics a natural woodland ecosystem. A food forest, however, focuses on edible trees, shrubs, perennials, and annuals. The food forest is a newer type of urban agriculture. It is not like a community garden system where people grow and harvest their own food. In a food forest, all food from the trees, bushes, and plants is available to anyone to eat for free. It's a public edible park. The primary goal is to provide healthy, affordable foods and enhance food security in lower income neighborhoods. Different versions of food forests appear in Portland, Syracuse, New York, Detroit, San Francisco, and Seattle. In Seattle, the city allocated money for the two-acre, phase-one development of The Beacon Hill Food Forest. The plans for the project now span seven acres. Community building and education are important aspects of the mission of a food forest. At the Beacon Hill Food Forest, fruit and nut trees make up the upper level, while berry shrubs, edible perennials and annuals make up the lower levels. There is even a "snack food" zone planted alongside an area where kids can play. Community volunteers known as "Friends of the Beacon Food Forest" coordinate for harvesting and maintenance of the edible plants (7-6).

Urban farming is more than vegetation. Seattle, Washington, long a leader in urban gardening allows up to eight domestic fowl on any city lot. With an Egg Handler/Dealer license from the Washington State Department of Agriculture people can legally sell eggs to retail outlets, and do not need a license to sell eggs from home directly to consumers. Seattle Tilth, an

7-6

7-7   7-8

organization that assists residents in growing their own food even offers chicken slaughtering classes, and many creative chicken coop concepts have emerged (7-7). The city also allows residents to have pygmy, dwarf, and miniature goats although with a few more restrictions than chickens.

In Melbourne, Australia, the harvesting of honey occurs on rooftops (7-8). In New York City, a 51-story building has 100,000 bees as tenants. Hives placed on commercial and residential rooftops in these cities produce honey sold within the city. Other major cities throughout the world, including San Francisco and Paris, are using rooftops, backyards and other city spaces to save honeybees, which suffer from Colony Collapse Disorder (CCD) and other maladies. Bees, those tireless workers, provide a critical service to the world in the form of plant pollination. Without this function most plants cannot reproduce, which could have a potentially devastating impact on agriculture and wild plants.

Provide Energy Options

Overly dependent on fossil fuels for decades, policies and practices promoting energy efficiency and renewable energy technologies are growing at exponential rates. While the most cost-efficient way of reducing energy use is the *negawatt*—energy not used because of conservation and energy efficiency—there are many other ways of reducing reliance on fossil fuels. These include incorporating passive systems within buildings based on ancient building typologies and using the latest advances in mechanical and control systems. Public acceptance of renewable energy options from the sun and wind is also advancing quickly as the costs come down. Although we aren't yet in the position to completely jettison fossil fuels such as natural gas to power cities, they should be considered "transitional fuels" until we can. There are just too many negative ramifications, both local and global, to continue our dependency on fossil fuels.

Capture the Sun

It was in 1931, in conversation with the industrialists, Henry Ford and Harvey Firestone, that Thomas Edison, the man most responsible for the advent of electricity, prophetically said, "We are like tenant farmers chopping down the fence around our house for fuel when we should be using Nature's inexhaustible sources of energy – sun, wind, and tide. I'd put my money on the sun and solar energy. What a source of power! I hope we don't have to wait until oil and coal run out before we tackle that." Fortunately, the use of renewables such as solar is growing, but not fast enough.

Modular installations using solar panels can be any size from a small residential rooftop system to an enormous hotel complex roof or a huge solar park. As this Bloomberg chart shows, the cost of solar photovoltaic (PV) cells is rapidly decreasing (7-9). Bolstered by the decline in prices, global solar PV capacity grew by 32% in 2017 according to a report by the International Renewable Energy Agency (IRENA) and Bloomberg New Energy Finance. The greatest growth is in China.

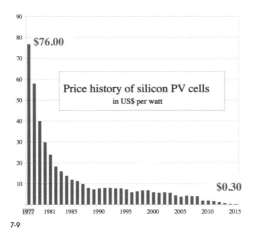

7-9

Many miles from China in the Andalusian countryside near Seville, Spain a collection of 600 mirrors and solar panels track the Sun's rays throughout the day. These rays strike heat exchangers at the top of the 40- and 50-story concrete towers. The illumination by the sun of the water vapor and dust in the air creates beams of white light that make the towers seem more like a religious pilgrimage destination than a power plant. One almost expects to hear ecclesiastical music bursting forth when the sun emerges on a cloudy day (7-10). Solar energy is the cleanest form of energy at any scale but photovoltaic solar panels, which generate electricity, have often been cost prohibitive. This solar power plant, and others like it, rely on conventional technologies used in novel ways. The light from the flat movable mirrors, called heliostats, and solar panels concentrates into heat exchangers, which transfer enough heat, 500°C, for water to turn to steam. The steam then powers turbines coupled with generators to produce electricity. When complete, the Seville project will include one more tower and five adjacent power plants. The plan is for the solar complex to meet Seville's residential energy needs (about 180,000 homes) without producing any greenhouse gas emissions.

The Crescent Dunes Solar Energy Project in Tonopah, Nevada has the capacity to provide 500,000 MW hours of electricity annually to 75,000 homes during peak demand (7-11). The 110 MW plant uses molten salt to store solar energy so electricity is available even when the sun is not shining. This flexibility contributes to the stability of the electrical grid. In this way, solving one problem (providing clean energy) does not contribute to another problem (stressing water resources). Crescent Dunes uses a highly efficient cooling power system to minimize water use.

When people think of Germany, they might not think of the solar capital of the world, and yet on a hot day, 50% of the country's electricity can come from solar, 90% of it from rooftop installations. The German model relies heavily on government subsidies and robust marketing campaigns to meet its solar targets with the goal of reducing coal use and eliminating nuclear power. In Freiburg, Germany a neighborhood uses large solar arrays on rooftops to produce its electricity (7-12). The solar arrays overhang the roof providing sun shading to the buildings.

7-10

7-11

162

7-12   7-13

Big Bellies, recycling and garbage receptacles found in many down-town centers, such as Washington, D.C. now feature solar panels on top which provide the power for compaction when sensors tell the bin it is close to full. With compaction, Big Bellies can hold up to eight times more garbage than similar sized bins. Sensors also send an electronic message to the public works department when the Big Belly needs emptying. This bin from near Edinburgh, Scotland even provides plastic bags for cleaning up after dogs (7-13).

Harvest the Wind

While airflow has ventilated spaces inhabited by humans since the days of living in caves, there has never been the mass harvesting of air currents that we find today. For centuries wind turbines have ground grain on farms. Now most wind turbines generate electricity. No longer the quaint windmills of yesteryear, wind turbines reach as tall as a 42-story building with blades over 200 feet long (making the transport of turbines and blades a challenge) (7-14). As of 2017, the largest wind turbine can power 7,500 homes. In Europe, wind powers the equivalent of 73 million households. In Spain in 2014, wind met 59% of the total power demand of the country (although this was a record). This meant that wind power prevented over 608 million tons of CO_2 emissions. In Copenhagen the distance from energy production to

7-14

7-15

Supporting People

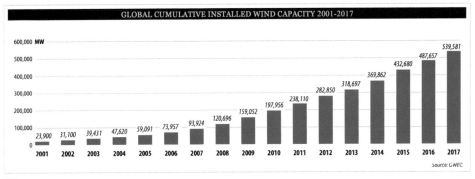

Source: GWEC

7-16

use is short. The wind turbines in the harbor present a unique joint owner-ship between the utility and thousands of customers who opted to invest, and share in the profits (7-15). The chart below by the Global Wind Energy Council shows the global growth in wind energy (7-16).

Nature as a Design Partner
Sometimes we need relief when there is too much light and heat. Humans are very responsive to changes in temperature and lighting. Even small children quickly figure out that it is cooler to move under the shade of a tree than stand under the sun. Designs of traditional buildings were responsive to temperature and light but when artificial heating, cooling, and lighting became standard in modern construction, these factors became less important. However, interest in reducing building energy is growing. According to the U.S. Department of Energy (DOE), in 2010 on average the building sector accounted for 41% of greenhouse gasses produced in the U.S. This is greater than the transportation or industrial sectors. A study focused on Chicago found that 70% of greenhouse emissions came from buildings as compared to 21% from cars and trucks.

Reducing temperature fluctuations on exterior walls impacts both the interior temperature of a building, as well as the temperature of the surrounding environment. A 1989 study in Oregon conducted by Luvall and Holbo demonstrated reductions of heat on exterior walls from 122°F to 77°F. One way to accomplish this is through green walls. Green walls have multiple benefits in addition to mitigating temperature fluctuations, including decreasing adjacent street level air pollution by as much as 40%

for nitrogen dioxide and 60% for particulate matter, as well as increasing biodiversity. Green walls can also provide a sense of delight. The whimsical living painting growing at the Universidad del Claustro de Sor Juana, in the historic center of Mexico City (7-17), includes the incorporation of a bicycle as shown in the close-up (7-18).

Another example of a clever design partnership with natural processes comes from Melbourne, Australia. Council House II, also known as CH2, is home to the Melbourne City Council and offers a stunning example of green building possibilities. Utilizing the physics of convection, the building has a ceiling of pre-cast wavy concrete that absorbs the rising hot air from the building until flushed at night through fanciful bright yellow ventilation stacks (7-19). By opening these "purge windows" for four hours at night during the summer, the building reduces its cooling requirements by 20%. Cooler air moves down the ventilation stacks to pre-condition the building for the workday. Chilled water contributes to the cooling through pipes that run through the beams and ceiling panels. Plants and other features also contribute to shading and cooling the building. CH2's vertical timber shutters provide full shading in the summer, while still allowing for filtered daylight and views. The recycled timber louvers and perforated metal sun-shading systems are part of a much larger design to provide daylighting while keeping the building cool in Melbourne's hot climate.

The Nykredit building in Copenhagen is an energy efficient building that uses computer-controlled sunshades to offset the great heat absorption potential of its massive glass facade. The glazing, which provides a comfortable naturally lit work environment and stunning views for employees also benefits the city by being an attractive addition to the civic landscape that looks very different depending on whether it is sunny or cloudy (7-20, 7-21). The Nykredit building also incorporates dappled sunscreens developed through the exciting field of biomimicry: the creation of products and techniques based on nature (7-22). Noticing how leaves on trees filter sunlight, biomimicry engineers created screens that would provide the same dappled effect for buildings.

Ancient history has much to teach us about using nature to keep indoor spaces comfortable with little or no energy. One example comes from hot, arid climates where wind towers, often in combination with small pools of

7-17

7-18

7-19

7-20

7-21

7-22

7-23

7-24

Supporting People

water to enhance the effect, naturally ventilate buildings (7-23). Originating in Persia and spreading to West Asia, this technique is being rediscovered for modern applications such as in the Zion National Park Visitors Center (7-24). The park uses towers with water spraying mechanisms that cool the air, causing it to sink and exit through the openings at the bottom of the tower. The flowing air causes the cooling effect.

Focus on Water

Although this section focuses on water and the previous one on energy, the reality is that water and energy are inextricably linked. Transporting, distributing, and purifying water used four percent of all electricity generated in the U.S. Up to 40% of electricity consumed in mid-sized cities is for pumping and aerating water.

Just as we take turning on the lights with the flip of a switch for granted, many of us in wealthier nations take water for granted. Clean, healthful water seems so available we even flush our toilets with it. However, water is more precious than we realize. There will never be any more of it on Earth than exists right now and 99% of it is economically inaccessible (e.g., in salt water or glaciers). For much of the world, water is a necessity that is already becoming scarce. According to a 2006 United Nations report, 1.8 billion people will be living in countries or regions with water scarcity, and two thirds of the world population could be under water stress conditions by 2025. Even in the United States, we are starting to see water shortages in southern states facing persistent drought like California. As Benjamin Franklin said, "When the well is dry, we learn the worth of water."

Stormwater Management

Managing stormwater flows in a city has become a bigger priority as urban waterways and the larger seas they flow into become more polluted. To reduce the costs associated with managing water while providing more public amenities, there is a toolkit of possibilities that cities can adapt to their own situations – many involve the integration of nature in the city.

Sometimes cities experience too much water at a time, such as during heavy rains. Enter green roofs. The plants on green roofs absorb

7-26

7-25

water, utilize it for metabolic processes, and return it to the atmosphere through transpiration. Green roofs not only retain rainwater (25% to 90% depending the roof depth and season), reducing the amount that enters a city's sewer system, but the roof's natural materials act as filters for any water that does run off. Green roofs come in all shapes and sizes including roofs planted with trees that serve as sky parks. These types of green roofs require a robust building structure to carry the weight of the heavy soil and plants. Alternatively, it takes just two inches of soil to construct relatively inexpensive green roofs using drought resistant lightweight sedums and mosses (7-25). Although most green roofs appear on flat rooftops, the green roofs on the 8-House outside of Copenhagen show the possibility of using steep roofs (7-26).

In addition to stormwater management, green roofs provide some building insulation during both hot and cold seasons, reduce urban heat island effects, improve air quality, dampen noise, create habitat for small

Supporting People

creatures like insects and birds, and prolong the service life of the underlying roof structures. This is because most traditional roofing materials degrade from fluctuations in temperature and sun exposure. Green roofs mitigate these impacts. Green roofs also provide a dynamic aesthetic element as many of the plants change colors with the seasons and can incorporate gardens or other appealing spaces accessible to building residents or the public. The view from a building in Potsdamerplatz, the former "no-man's land" between East and West Berlin, shows how much nicer it is to look down on green roofs than on typical black tar roofs (7-27).

Another way to mitigate stormwater impacts is with pervious or permeable pavement that allows rainwater to filter through the road material to the ground (7-28). This approach to paving has many benefits particularly when part of an overall stormwater management system. Allowing water to filter down into the soil rather than pooling on hard surfaces reduces the amount of water flowing into combined sewage and stormwater systems during heavy rains. This prevents overwhelmed systems from releasing raw sewage into natural urban waterways. Pervious pavement filters solids and pollutants out of rainwater from vehicles, such as metals from brake pads and oil, decreasing the amount that is sloughed off into urban lakes, rivers, and creeks.

Another concept implemented in Nantes, France as well as other cities is the laying of tram tracks within a planted strip of roadway (7-29). Planting low growing plants between tramlines provides the benefits mentioned above with the addition of reducing noise.

In Seattle, Washington, a comprehensive approach called Green Stormwater Infrastructure (GSI) helps prevent polluted water from entering the many urban creeks, lakes, and the Puget Sound. GIS encompasses resource conservation and the use of natural features and systems, such as trees and shrubs, rain gardens, permeable pavement, bioswales, creek daylighting, and green roofs. Rainwater is also harvested. The focus on GSI as a Low Impact Development (LID) strategy originated because polluted stormwater runoff would drain directly from the streets into creek basins throughout the city, draining into local freshwater lakes and the Puget Sound. Seattle's first set of GSI projects, completed from 2001 to 2006, focused on creek basins in areas without piped drainage systems. These

7-27

7-28

7-29

Supporting People

7-30

projects proved highly effective, in some cases reducing creek pollutants up to 99%. The cost of implementing GSI solutions is less than the cost of traditional pipe systems, which requires digging up the streets. Mimicking the natural environment, GSI solutions in urban neighborhoods provide wildlife habitat for small creatures and birds and a living laboratory for children to explore. Often, more green space contributes to higher home values such as in the Seattle neighborhood Belltown (7-30).

Another approach to stormwater mitigation is from Curitiba, Brazil. Curitiba's humid subtropical highland climate and its location on a flat plateau with multiple rivers subjected the city to frequent stormwater events and flooding. Its rapid growth and urbanization increased the amount of impervious surfaces and degraded water quality. The city lacked the financial resources to construct large water treatment plants and, as with other challenges, relied on creativity and intelligence rather than money to come up solutions that provided multiple benefits. To mitigate the pollutant load on its many rivers and streams, to decrease pervasive flooding, and to reduce water treatment costs, the city developed over 5,000 acres of parks and green spaces along its rivers, planting millions of trees and building small dams and new lakes. This extensive park network functions as an effective and natural stormwater system. When flooding occurs, the lakes act as holding basins. Overflow, when it occurs, drains into the surrounding parks, not inhabited areas. One section of the park network, Tanguá Park (7-31), inaugurated in 1996, transformed several former quarries into a series of lakes with a stunning waterfall surrounded by greenspace and an abundance of park amenities. The lake levels rise and fall depending on the amount of rainfall.

Another city that has combined recreational and stormwater functions but in a much different way than Curitiba is Roskilde, Denmark. With climate change, Denmark has experienced a series of flash floods costing over US $1 billion in damage. An innovative solution to manage stormwater while providing people with recreational amenities is Rabalderparken, a large park built on a former industrial site previously occupied by a concrete factory. Today Rabalderparken includes, among other amenities, a skateboard park that serves as an integrated drainage canal (7-32). In total, the Raldenparken's stormwater drainage system can hold up to 23,000 cubic meters, or 10 Olympic-size swimming pools of rainwater.

Malmö, Sweden has taken a contemporary design approach to managing stormwater. Built on the land of the former shipyard, the Bo01 section of Västra Hamnen (Western Harbor in English) is an ecologically sustainable neighborhood. One of its key features is its comprehensive natural stormwater system that starts on rooftops with green roofs and continues with runoff guided by attractive channels in the streets that lead to various fountains and ponds and ultimately into a large canal that goes to the sea (7-33, 7-34). Another Malmö neighborhood, Augustenborg, an older neighborhood redeveloped to be more sustainable, utilizes an even more natural aesthetic rather than the modern design aesthetic used in Västra Hamnen (7-35).

Supporting People

7-31

7-32

175

7-33

7-34

7-35

Supporting People

Bring Nature into the City

As should be apparent from the examples above, nature protects, supports, and nourishes a city's environment and its people. The co-benefits of bringing nature into a city are extraordinary. Trees, parks, and greenery help to clean the air and water by trapping particulate pollutants such as dust, ash, smoke, and pollen and absorbing carbon dioxide and other gases, then replenishing the atmosphere with oxygen. Nature in urban spaces cools cities by reducing the "heat island" effect caused by an abundance of concrete, steel, and asphalt. Urban greenery dampens noise, reduces wind speeds, and provides habitat to wildlife and pollinators that are part of larger regional ecosystems. Nature is the perfect partner in water management, retaining and filtering stormwater through the daylighting or creation of more surface creek channels, rain gardens, swales, planted curb extensions, green roofs, and other techniques.

A great example of this partnership is Dockside Green in Victoria, B.C. This mixed-use urban neighborhood boasts an environmentally sustainable infrastructure that not only integrates nature, but educates people about water management in the process. Residents and visitors see how water absorbs into rain gardens, green roofs, and permeable pavement and flows through a system of terraced ponds and creeks that together create a central neighborhood greenway and attractive public space, rich with wetland plants and attractive to wildlife (7-36).

And there's more. People are healthier both physically and mentally from cleaner air and from increased activity such as walking, playing in the park, and urban gardening, all of which green spaces encourage. Researchers have also documented an array of social and psychological benefits that being around nature and greenery promote. These range from lower stress levels, higher creative output, more social interaction and children's play, as well as a greater appreciation for the natural world, in general. Urban trees and greenery can add character, define spaces, create intimacy, and even protect us from cars.

We know, for example, that city residents with little or no access to greenery have higher rates of psychological problems and stress hormones than people who live closer to nature or have ready access to parks, gardens,

7-36

7-37   7-38

or even greenery in planters. Neighborhoods with higher ratios of greenery have children with lower excess weight gain and rates of asthma. Research in the Netherlands found that the greener the neighborhood, the less prevalence of 16 different medical conditions in adults, such as joint pain, depression, diabetes, and headaches. In Tokyo (7-37), researchers found that the elderly who have access to urban parks and tree-lined streets have longer survival rates.

Access to nature in the city is also an issue of social justice. Research confirms that the presence of nature corresponds to income levels in urban areas. In cities ranging from Seattle to Adelaide to Beijing higher-income neighborhoods boast significantly more tree cover and bird diversity than lower-incomes areas, regardless of the age of those neighborhoods. In Los Angeles, lower-income areas and neighborhoods of color have lower levels of per capita park access. The most dramatic documentation of these inequities come from satellite images from Google Earth of low-SES versus high-SES neighborhoods documenting the lack of trees in the low-SES neighborhoods. To help change this, volunteers in communities from Richmond, California to West Baltimore's Franklin Square plant fruit trees and gardens in a neighborhood in need of a little green and fresh food. (7-38).

Connecting People to Nature

Botanists and environmental and wildlife scientists who specialize in urban areas say that one major obstacle they face is the myth that there is no nature in cities. To the contrary, cities are complex ecological systems with diverse trees, vegetation, birds, insects, small mammals, and in many places fish and water systems. Increased public awareness is important because it's not just greenery that cities need, but biodiversity. It matters what types of trees or shrubbery gets planted. It matters how urban planners design, size, and shape parks, green patches or corridors. Cities, no matter how small, provide important ecosystem services in the face of climate change and widespread declines in numbers and diversity of species. Cities need the public to recognize that spending public monies to bring more nature in the city is not just for aesthetics.

One way to increase public awareness is to promote the use of plants on buildings for breeding, shelter and food for small creatures like insects and birds. One of the more spectacular examples of a 'living' building is Bosco Verticale (Vertical Forest) in Milan, Italy (7-39). This pair of residential towers support 730 trees, 5,000 shrubs, 11,000 groundcover and perennials on exterior facades. Botanists and horticulturalists worked closed with designer Boeri Studio to ensure that the structure could bear the load of the plants, as well as remain healthy and intact in winds. This award-winning and environmentally innovative building was a key element in the restoration of Milan's historic district.

On an even larger scale, between 1986 and 2007 Singapore grew in population by two million people, yet contrary to what one might expect satellite images show that the island increased in percentage of green space from 36 to 47%. How did that happen? The National Biodiversity Centre of the National Parks Board designed a national strategy, called the Community in Nature Initiative (CIN), to promote, educate, and involve citizens in nature conservation. CIN integrated nature-related activities in schools, including new curricula to learn about the benefits of biodiversity and hands-on activities for students such as the creation of bird and butterfly gardens. It offered tree-planting events, gardening workshops, nature walks, and other opportunities to get families involved with nature. CIN trained citizens in collecting data related to herons, seagrass, and bird migrations. The CIN initiative helped galvanize public support for a number of significant projects, such as the daylighting of the Kallang River in Bishan-Ang Mo Kio Park shown in this before and after photo (7-40).

7-36

Supporting People

In Seattle, an innovative project raised public awareness while building a key corridor for struggling non-human residents of that city: pollinators such as butterflies, birds, bats, and certain insects and bees. The Pollinator Pathways project started as a vision by artist and designer Sarah Bergmann in 2008 to highlight the loss of pollinators in urban environments. What resulted was the creation of a mile long functioning pollinator pathway, designed and supported through a non-profit community effort (7-41, 7-42). To launch this project, Bergmann drew a line on a map that connected two large green spaces in Seattle (a pesticide-free university campus and a

7-40

7-41

7-42

7-39

7-43

7-44

7-45

wooded area a mile away). Pollinator Pathway volunteers then identified underdeveloped spaces along that line, such as sidewalk strips, medians, rooftops, and homeowner yards, that could host native plants attractive to pollinators. In addition to working with the city and local universities, a key aspect of this project was to approach homeowners to participate. In many cases, the response was very enthusiastic. Homeowners could select from a list of 50 native plants. Bergmann would offer to design original gardens for their front strips with the expectation that homeowners would maintain them. The non-profit hosted planting parties and taught gardening skills. One resident claimed that it was a "mark of honor" to be part of the Pollinator Pathway and a positive activity to share with neighbors.

Another unique program designed to raise public awareness about urban trees took a highly unusual turn. The city of Melbourne started a program where it assigned urban trees ID numbers and email addresses so that citizens could easily report problems such as broken branches (7-43). Residents simply use their computer or smartphone to click on a tree on a Melbourne Urban Forest map, then send their message. To the surprise of city staff, people not only reported broken branches but wrote personal expressions of affection and thanks to the trees. One person wrote to an Algerian Oak: "Thank you for giving us oxygen. Thank you for being so pretty...Stay strong, stand tall..." Another sent a green-leaf elm this message: "As I was leaving St. Mary's College today I was struck, not by a branch, but by your radiant beauty...I have exams coming up and I should be busying studying." Staff members were so moved by the thousands of messages received that the "trees" started to answer back. The St. Mary's College student received a response from Green Elm Tree ID 1022165: "I hope you do well in your exams. Research has shown that nature can influence the way people learn in a positive way, so I hope I inspire your learning." As the Chair of Melbourne's Environment Portfolio stated, "The [email-a-tree program] reveals the love Melburnians have for our trees."

In Minneapolis, the city focused on connecting kids to nature by creating the Twin Cities Adventure Play park. The goal of this park is to encourage kids to have fun with limbs, sticks and stumps (7-44, 7-45). Kids (and parents) are free to build forts, create obstacle courses, or whatever creative ideas emerge when surrounded by nature's toys.

Wrapping up this chapter and this book's global tour, one of the most important trends we see is cities embracing the regenerative power of nature to improve urban livability and sustainability. When it comes to supporting people by providing basics such as food, energy, water, and public health, cities are rediscovering nature as a role model, design partner, educational tool, and cost-effective means to address these fundamental needs.

Photo Credits by Chapter

Cover

Front: Girls playing in Barcelona by Jim Mueller
Dockside Green, Victoria, B.C.: Courtesy of i-SUSTAIN
Art Lamp in Plaza, Malmo, Sweden by Jim Mueller

Back: People on 2nd Ave Seattle demonstration photo: Courtesy of OnRequest Images and i-SUSTAIN

Chapter 2: Inviting People

2-1 Yu Garden and Bazaar, Old Town, Shanghai, China (2009) by Lyn Gately (CC): https://www.flickr.com/photos/lyng883/4832039309/

2-2 Trastevere, Rome, Italy by Sergio Calleja (CC): http://www.flickr.com/photos/scalleja/760258817/

2-3 Laneway with graffiti, Melbourne, Australia by Alan Levine (CC): http://www.flickr.com/photos/37996646802@N01/1544152594

2-4 Renovated laneway Melbourne, Australia (2013) by Brian Giesen (CC): https://www.flickr.com/photos/briangiesen/4919302861/

2-5 Tree canopy with transit, Portland, Oregon (2011) by Ian Sane (CC): https://www.flickr.com/photos/31246066@N04/6475455261/in/album-72157617137856012/

2-6 SW Ankeny Street, Portland Oregon by Jaime Valdez, Portland Tribune: http://portlandtribune.com/pt/11-features/156811-ankeny-turns-on-party-lights

2-7 Bo01 aerial, Malmo, Sweden by Michael Bo Rasmussen

2-8 Bo01 street, Malmo, Sweden (2006): Courtesy of i-SUSTAIN

2-9 Vacuum system, Stockholm by Michael Bo Rasmussen

2-10 La Boca, Buenos Aires, Argentina (2010) by Chimpanz APe (CC): http://www.flickr.com/photos/52032399@N00/5189130749

2-11 Plaza, Leipzig, Germany (2008) by Christian Ludborzs (CC): http://www.flickr.com/photos/32967167@N06/3074592576

2-12 Wayfinding signage, London, England (2010) by Rob Brewer (CC): http://www.flickr.com/photos/rbrwr/4722416820

2-13 Dogs at crosswalk, NYC (2010) by c_pichler (CC): https://www.flickr.com/photos/30839999@N06/4335002328

2-14 Bike rain gutter, Enschede, Netherlands (2014) by Tim Fuller (CC): http://www.flickr.com/photos/11214828@N00/12271777125

2-15 Windblock, umbrellas and heat lamp, Cafe Flore, San Francisco by Helder Ribeiro from Campinas, Brazil (Cafe Floré) [CC BY-SA 2.0 (https://creativecommons.org/licenses/by-sa/2.0)], via Wikimedia Commons

2-16 Tree over pocket park, Stockholm, Sweden (2011) by Hans Willems (CC): http://www.flickr.com/photos/92451458@N07/8442925368

2-17 Shopping avenue, Malaga, Spain by Rosemary Dukelow (CC): http://www.flickr.com/photos/travelswithrosemary/4739427762/

2-18 Playing chess in Baku, Azerbaijan (2009) by Самый древний (CC) via Wikimedia Commons http://commons.wikimedia.org/wiki/File%3APlaying_chess_in_baku_Old_City.jpg

2-19 Closed sidewalk, St. Louis (2012) by Paul Sableman (CC): http://www.flickr.com/photos/53301297@N00/7978177488

2-20 Old Town Cartagena, Colombia (2011) by Joe Ross (CC): https://www.flickr.com/photos/joeross/24471270199/

2-21 Art Lamp, Malmo, Sweden by Jim Mueller

2-22 Cheonggyecheon fountain and lights via Wikimedia Commons (CC): http://en.wikipedia.org/wiki/File:Seoul_Cheonggyecheon_night.jpg

2-23 Row houses, Washington, D.C. (2011) by Wonderlane (CC): http://www.flickr.com/photos/71401718@N00/6401109277

2-24 Market, Istanbul, Turkey (2010) by Jim Mueller

2-25 Liege Guillemins railway station, Liege, Belgium (2010) by L'amande (CC): https://www.flickr.com/photos/54632345@N03/8116058772

2-26 Tree well pattern, Burlington, Vermont (2007) by NNECAPA Photo Library (CC): http://www.flickr.com/photos/nnecapa/2874145790

2-27 Wisteria climbing a historic building facade, Brussels, Belgium (2011) by La Citta Vita (CC): http://www.flickr.com/photos/49539505@N04/7202567182

2-28 Old City, Jerusalem (2008) by David Masters (CC): http://www.flickr.com/photos/25652278@N03/3056839532

2-29 Food Market, Hanoi, Vietnam (2009) by HoangP (CC): http://www.flickr.com/photos/25336133@N02/3829317623

2-30 Street musician, Vienna (2011) by Cha già José (CC): https://www.flickr.com/photos/chagiajose/6138190362/

2-31 Horse carriage, Bruges, Belgium (2009) by Kelley McCarthy (CC): https://www.flickr.com/photos/79505158@N00/4108367677

2-32 Kuala Lumpur Street Festival, Malaysia (2014) by John Ragai (CC):
https://www.flickr.com/photos/40642065@N06/13510533364

2-33 Performers on stilts, Havana Cuba (2009) by Jim Mueller

2-34 Opera on La Rambla, Barcelona, Spain courtesy of i-SUSTAIN

2-35 Dancing the Sardana, Barcelona (2008) by Alan Mayers via Wikimedia Commons [CC BY-SA 2.0 (https://creativecommons.org/licenses/by-sa/2.0)]

2-36 Cinema in the park, Pittsburgh, Pennsylvania by City of Pittsburgh Parks Department (CC):
pittsburghpa.gov/citiparks/cinema-in-park⬚

2-37 Leichhardt Park, Sydney (2012) by Dushan Hanuska (CC):
http://www.flickr.com/photos/hanuska/7123665385

2-38 Exercisers, Shanghai, China courtesy of i-SUSTAIN

2-39 Taichi in Beijing park (2010) by Keith Yahl (CC): http://www.flickr.com/photos/yahl/11475372393/

2-40 Table Tennis in park, Paris, France by Chris Winters (CC):
https://www.flickr.com/photos/cwinters/29670314718/

2-41 Waterski in front of waste-to-energy plant, Copenhagen, Denmark by Michael Bo Rasmussen

2-42 Mixed-use Friedrichshain, Berlin (2011) by Citta Vita (CC)
https://www.flickr.com/photos/la-citta-vita/5852478849/

2-43 Mixed-use neighborhood, Bitola, Republic of Macedonia (2007) by Revizionist (CC) via Wikimedia Commons
http://en.wikipedia.org/wiki/File:Bitola_2007.JPG

2-44 Japanese women on bench by MrHicks46 (CC) sourced at:
http://www.psypost.org/2014/03/boosting-self-esteem-prevents-health-problems-for-seniors-23651#pretty-Photo/0/

2-45 Smooth strip in sidewalk, Potsdam, Germany (2013) by Alper Çugun (CC)
http://www.flickr.com/photos/12505664@N00/9444401568

2-46 Elderly woman on stairs, New York City (2009) by H.L.I.T (CC):
http://www.flickr.com/photos/29311691@N05/3336703576/

2-47 Man on bench, Lisbon, Portugal (2011) by Michael Coghlan (CC):
https://www.flickr.com/photos/89165847@N00/5960543717

2-48 Elderly woman crossing road, New York City (2008) by Ed Yourdon (CC):
http://www.flickr.com/photos/72098626@N00/3050394176

2-49 Median refuge, Washington, D.C. (2011) by Payton Chung (CC): https://www.flickr.com/photos/paytonc/5352815463/

2-50 Tram ramp, Poland by Lasart75 (CC): http://en.wikipedia.org/wiki/File:Protram205_ramp.JPG

2-51 Storefront, St. Jacobs, Ontario, Canada (2011) by Allie Caulfield (CC):
https://www.flickr.com/photos/28577026@N02/6066551389

2-52 Seniors seeking shade, Chile (2006) by Peter Merholz (CC):
http://www.flickr.com/photos/35468145500@N01/294058768

2-53 Intergenerational garden, Washington, D.C. by Ted Eytan (CC):
https://www.flickr.com/photos/taedc/5493770237/

2-54 Assistance for Blind, Kyoto-shi, Japan (2012) by Jason Riedy (CC):
http://www.flickr.com/photos/jason-riedy/6883248388/

2-55 Wheelchair swing, Tamworth, Australia by Tamworth Regional Council (CC):
http://www.tamworth.nsw.gov.au/Community/Aged-and-Disability-Services/

2-56 Children playing street hockey, Vancouver, BC, Canada (2005) by Pete (originally posted to Flickr as determination_0970) [CC BY-SA 2.0 (https://creativecommons.org/licenses/by-sa/2.0)], via Wikimedia Commons

2-57 Children playing in water, Davis, CA (2005) by Bev Sykes (CC):
http://en.wikipedia.org/wiki/Childhood#mediaviewer/File:Fountain_Fun.jpg

2-58 Girl Play Streets Program, New York City by NYC Healthy Neighborhoods (CC):
http://nychealthyneighborhoods.tumblr.com/post/92731998360/

2-59 Little girl participating in cicLAvia, Los Angeles, California (2011) by Umberto Brayj (CC):
http://www.flickr.com/photos/ubrayj02/6227856389

2-60 Ramona Apartments, Portland, Oregon by RentCafe (CC):
https://www.rentcafe.com/apartments/or/portland/ramona-apartments-0/default.aspx

Chapter 3: Inspiring People

3-1 Teapot Garden by unknown (CC): posted at https://www.facebook.com/karolina.l.pawelec

3-2 Mosaic trash bin, Charlotte, North Carolina (2007) by James Willamor (CC):
https://www.flickr.com/photos/bz3rk/3823807499

3-3 Bongo trash cans, Curitiba, Brazil (2006) by Jim Mueller

3-4 Fish downspout, Madrid, Spain (2012) by Jim Mueller

3-5 Cactus painted drain pipe, Vitoria-Gasteiz, Spain (2011) by Zarateman [CC0], from Wikimedia Commons
http://commons.wikimedia.org/wiki/File%3AVitoria_-_Graffiti_%26_Murals_0890.JPG

3-6 Dublin utility box (bookshelf design) (2013) by William Murphy (CC):
www.flickr.com/photos/infomatique/7321803482/

3-7 Painted power cabinet, Auckland, New Zealand vy Ingolfson [Public domain], from Wikimedia Commons
http://commons.wikimedia.org/wiki/File:Power_Cabinet_With_Nice_Art_On_It.jpg

3-8 Manhole cover (squid), Hakodate, Japan (2005) by Toby Oxborrow (CC):
https://www.flickr.com/photos/oxborrow/53034599/

3-9 Melbourne street furniture courtesy of i-SUSTAIN

3-10 Orange bike rack, Rzeszow, Poland (2012) by Zorro2212 [CC BY-SA 3.0 (https://creativecommons.org/licenses/by-sa/3.0)], from Wikimedia Commons
http://commons.wikimedia.org/wiki/File:Bike_racks_in_Rzesz%C3%B3w.jpg

3-11 Typographic bus stop, Baltimore by mmmm....(CC):
https://www.designboom.com/art/mmmm-bus-stop-baltimore-08-07-2014/

3-12 Public toilet, West Bromwich, England (2011) by Elliott Brown (CC):
https://www.flickr.com/photos/ell-r-brown/5585737824/

3-13 Kawakawa, New Zealand Hundertwasser toilet (outside) by W. Bulach via Wikimedia Commons
https://nl.wikipedia.org/wiki/Bestand:0_3060Kawakawa_-_Neuseeland_-_Hundertwassertoilette.jpg

3-14 Ponyfish Island, bar under the bridge, Melbourne, Australia:
https://whatson.melbourne.vic.gov.au/DiningandNightlife/BarsandPubs/AllBars/Pages/7362.aspx:

3-15 Paris Plages (2009) by slasher-fun (CC) via Wikimedia Commons
http://en.wikipedia.org/wiki/File:Paris_plage_3.jpg

3-16 Surfing in Eisbach River, Munich, Germany (2014) by Gabler-Werbung (CC):
http://pixabay.com/en/eisbach-munich-english-garden-293792/

3-17 The Blue Lagoon Spa, Iceland by Prosthetic Head - Own work, CC BY-SA 4.0, https://commons.wikimedia.org/w/index.php?curid=48297823

3-18 Opera House, Oslo, Norway (2008) courtesy of Visit OSLO:
https://www.flickr.com/photos/35811945@N05/5555503102/

3-19 Rooftop Bar and Cinema, Melbourne (2009) by Alpha (CC)
https://www.flickr.com/photos/10559879@N00/4139546949

3-20 Waste-to-energy ski hill photo courtesy of BIG-Bjarke Ingels Group

3-21 Rooftop farm, JR Ebisu train station, Tokyo Japan, fastcoexist.com (CC):
http://www.fastcoexist.com/3027821/no-time-to-garden-at-home-at-this-train-station-you-can-garden-on-your-commute

3-22 Woman in swing at bus stop, London, England by Bruno Taylor
http://www.pixelsumo.com/post/bruno-taylor

3-23 Bellevue Square Park, Kensington Market, Toronto by Josephers (CC) via Wikimedia Commons
http://en.wikipedia.org/wiki/File:People_scenery_at_Bellevue_Square_Park_in_Kensington_Market,_Toronto.jpg

3-24 Elburg, Netherlands (2014) by bertknot (CC): https://www.flickr.com/photos/bertknot/15609909989/

3-25 Campo de' Fiori (day), Rome, Italy by Lynsey Newton (CC):
http://narrativelyspeaking.blogspot.com/2013/09/a-little-too-far-blog-tour-and-giveaway.html

3-26 Campo dd' Fiori (evening), Rome, Italy (2005) by Sergio Calleja (CC):
https://www.flickr.com/photos/24899877@N00/103029370

3-27 Marché aux Puces, Saint Quen, Paris, France (2013) by Juan Antonio Segal (CC)
https://www.flickr.com/photos/jafsegal/8496543917/

3-28 Ciclovia, Avenida Reforma, Mexico City, Mexico by Katie Bordner (CC):
https://www.flickr.com/photos/katiebordner/33922656616/

3-29 Make Sunday Special Water slide, Bristol, UK (2014) by George Ferguson

3-30 Free Tango, Vancouver B.C., Canada courtesy of VIVA Vancouver
https://www.facebook.com/VivaVancouver/photos_stream

3-31 McCormick Tribune Plaza (summer), Chicago, Illinois (2013) by Ken Lund (CC)
https://www.flickr.com/photos/75683070@N00/9181705672

3-32 McCormick Tribune Plaza (winter), Chicago, Illinois by Flickr user laffy4k - https://www.flickr.com/photos/
laffy4k/67843322/, CC BY 2.0, https://commons.wikimedia.org/w/index.php?curid=4250610

3-33 Artwork "Propioception," artist Hannah Quinn Rivenburgh, Minneapolis, MN (2014) by Steven Lang,
Courtesy of Hennepin Theater Trust

3-34 Girls playing with metal ball, Barcelona (2012) by Jim Mueller

3-35 Man playing with metal ball, Barcelona (2012) by Jim Mueller

3-36 Pissing dog sculpture (the Zinneke), Brussels by Maxifred - Own work, CC BY-SA 3.0, https://commons.
wikimedia.org/w/index.php?curid=19471190

3-37 Chalk art by David Zinn: http://www.cuded.com/2013/01/playful-chalk-art-by-david-zinn/

3-38 Glasgow (Mitchell street) mural, "Honey I Shrunk the Kids" by Smug, Scotland by Thomas Nugent
(CC-by-sa/2.0) http://www.geograph.org.uk/photo/3022163

3-39 High Line, New York by David Berkowitz (CC): https://www.flickr.com/photos/davidberkowitz/5923527436/

3-40 Sunflowers Brussels by brusselsfarmer2 (CC): https://www.flickr.com/photos/brusselsfarmer/941764661/

3-41 Whoopdeedoo ramp, Vancouver, BC, Canada (2013) by Paul Krueger (CC):
https://www.flickr.com/photos/pwkrueger/8897331142/

3-42 Yarn bomb - Madrid, Spain (2011) by Alvario León (CC):
http://commons.wikimedia.org/wiki/File:Yarn_Bombing_Bolardos_by_Teje_La_Ara%C3%B1a_2.jpg

3-43 Installing a Red Swing, Austin, Texas (2010) by Gideon Tsang (CC):
https://www.flickr.com/photos/gideon/5210145087

3-44 Two girls on 21 Swings, Montreal, Canada by Quartier des Spectacles:
https://www.flickr.com/photos/quartierdesspectacles/5665905362/

3-45 Appearing Rooms Fountain, Forrest Place, Perth, Australia by Jeppe Hein (CC); http://www.jeppehein.net

3-46 Crown Fountain, Millennium Park, Chicago, Illinois by Roman Boed (CC):
https://www.flickr.com/photos/romanboed/35529635983

3-47 Crown Fountain Kids. City of Chicago:
https://www.cityofchicago.org/city/en/depts/dca/supp_info/millennium_park_-crownfountainfactsfigures.html

3-48 Urban treasure hunt stop (clue 47), Copenhagen, Denmark (2009) by Jane Mejdahl (CC):
https://www.flickr.com/photos/gullig/3766226669

Chapter 4: Connecting People

4-1 Old Town Square, Prague, Czech Republic (2009) by Kham Tran (CC):
https://www.flickr.com/photos/khamtran/3766284781/

4-2 Federation Square by Jorge Láscar from Australia - Federation Square, CC BY 2.0, https://commons.
wikimedia.org/w/index.php?curid=31949778

4-3 Federation Square (Kevin Rudd apology) (2008) by Virginia Murdoch (CC):
https://www.flickr.com/photos/virginiam/2261163403/

4-4 The Phillips West Neighborhood National Night Out, Minneapolis, MN (2006) by Tony Webster (CC):
https://www.flickr.com/photos/diversey/229020018/

4-5 Chess beach, Santa Monica, CA (2011) by InSapphoWeTrust (CC):
http://www.flickr.com/photos/56619626@N05/5847210765

4-6 Pedestrian area, Jerusalem, Israel (2004) by Jim Mueller

4-7 MoMa sculpture garden, New York City (2010) by La Citta Vita (CC):
http://www.flickr.com/photos/la-citta-vita/4545264454/

4-8 Abingdon Square Park (2008) by Naked Pictures of Bea Arthur CC BY-SA 3.0, https://commons.wikimedia.
org/w/index.php?curid=5048629

4-9 Noriega Street Parklet (2012) by San Francisco Planning Department (CC):
http://www.flickr.com/photos/sfplanning/8456346389/

4-10 Modified Social Benches by artist Jeppe Hein: http://www.jeppehein.net/pages/publics.php

4-11 Dog Park, Baltimore Parks and Recreation (CC):
http://www.flickr.com/photos/bmorerecnparks/8280387347/

4-12 Tool Library, Toronto, Canada (2014) by the Institute for a Resource-Based Economy (CC):
https://www.flickr.com/photos/toollibrary/14427641289

4-13 Urbana Illinois MakerSpace (2012) by Mitch Altman (CC):
https://www.flickr.com/photos/maltman23/6954963687

4-14 Sunnyside Piazza, Portland OR by The City Repair Project

4-15 Free wood, Shoreline, Washington (2009) by Wonderlane (CC): https://www.flickr.com/photos/
wonderlane/3878640866

4-16 Twilight Hawkers Market, Perth (2015) by Sally Lewis, Events & Beyond

4-17 Food trucks in Portland by star511 (CC): https://www.flickr.com/photos/johnjoh/6147400329/in/photostream/

4-18 Gilroy Garlic Festival (2007) by Eric Chan (CC): https://www.flickr.com/photos/maveric2003/934051208/

4-19 Cheonggyecheon Highway 1969 by Seoul Metropolitan Government - Seoul Metropolitan Government, CC BY-SA 4.0, https://commons.wikimedia.org/w/index.php?curid=39939914

4 20 Cheonggyecheon stream, Seoul, South Korea (2010) by Jessica Gardner (CC): https://www.flickr.com/photos/pjgardner/4615685290/

4-21 Memorial of Murdered Jews (2005) by Jim Mueller

4-22 Berlin wall fragment (2005) by Jim Mueller

4-23 Berlin Street Scene (2011) by La Citta Vita (CC): https://www.flickr.com/photos/la-citta-vita/5852473107/

4-24 Hot Metal Bridge, Three Rivers Heritage Trail (2009) by Ian Norman (CC): https://www.flickr.com/photos/inorman/3471520325/

4-25 Turning Torso, Malmo, Sweden, courtesy of i-SUSTAIN

4-26 and 27 Royal Danish Academy of Fine Arts architectural studios by Michael Bo Rasmussen

4-28 Gemini Apartments, Copenhagen Denmark (2012) by Rob Deutscher (CC) https://www.flickr.com/photos/bobarc/7988027082/

4-29 Mexico City, Zocalo Station by Xuan Che (CC): https://www.flickr.com/photos/rosemania/348334161

4-30 The Sisyphers gnomes, Wroclaw (statue artist Tomasz Moczek) (2013) by Tomasz MoczekPnapora [CC BY-SA 3.0 (https://creativecommons.org/licenses/by-sa/3.0)], from Wikimedia Commons By Pnapora (CC)

4-31 Gnomes of Wroclaw (chained gnome) 2011 by Paul (CC): https://www.flickr.com/photos/paul1/6286744603/

4-32 "Little horse, Portland, Oregon" (2009) by piddix via Wikimedia Commons (CC): http://commons.wikimedia.org/wiki/File:Little_horse,_Portland,_Oregon.jpg#/media/File:Little_horse,_Portland,_Oregon.jpg

4-33 Baby Jumping, Castrillo de Murcia (2008) by Jtspotau - Own work, (CC) BY 3.0, https://en.wikipedia.org/wiki/Baby_jumping#/media/File:Colacho_salto_danzantes_03250.jpg

4-34 Castellers, Lleida, Spain (2009) by Montserrat Torres - Castellers de la Vila de Gràcia, CC BY 3.0, https://commons.wikimedia.org/w/index.php?curid=8351765

4-35 Powderhorn 24 bike race checkpoint punch, Minneapolis, MN (2012) by Tony Webster (CC): https://www.flickr.com/photos/diversey/7424242046/

4-36 Jaimanitas Neighborhood mosaics (2010), courtesy of i-SUSTAIN

4-37 Meet the Streets festival, NYC (2009) NYC DOT (CC): https://www.flickr.com/photos/nycstreets/4029326531/

4-30 Adams Morgan sign, courtesy of i-SUSTAIN

4-39 Rainier Valley hyper local radio on National Radio Day event (2015), courtesy of Seattle.gov
http://techtalk.seattle.gov/2015/08/20/nationalradioday-a-success-in-seattle/

4-40 Neighborhood walking tour in Seattle, Washington, courtesy of Feet First, Feetfirst.org

4-41 Portland China Gate, Old Town, Portland, Oregon (2007) by Noël Zia Lee (CC):
https://www.flickr.com/photos/noelzialee/651214885

4-42 Stargazing in Davis, CA (2014) by Danielle Buma (CC):
https://www.flickr.com/photos/-elleinad-/13964109141/

Chapter 5: Communicating with People

5-1 Calle Francisco I. Madero, Mexico, 2007 (before) CC BY-SA 2.5
https://no.wikipedia.org/wiki/Calle_Francisco_I._Madero#/media/File:Avenida_Madero_Mexico_Centro_
Historico.jpg

5-2 Calle Francisco I. Madero (after) by Fribae [CC BY-SA 3.0 (https://creativecommons.org/licenses/by-sa/3.0)],
from Wikimedia Commons

5-3 Second Ave Bike Lane Demonstration Project (2014) SDOT Photos (CC):
https://www.flickr.com/photos/sdot_photos/14994730679

5-4 London Chair Experiment: http://cargocollective.com/urbanexperiments/100-Chairs-Experiment

5-5 London Grass Experiment: http://cargocollective.com/urbanexperiments/Grass-Experiment

5-6 Smart Crosswalk: https://www.mirror.co.uk/news/uk-news/high-tech-pedestrian-crossing-lights-11310678

5-7 Day without Cars, Paris Promotional Poster: https://s1.cdn.autoevolution.com/images/news/gallery/paris-
will-be-completely-free-of-traffic-for-one-lucky-day-in-september_1.jpeg

5-8 Tegg Grasslands, Melbourne: https://blogs.slv.vic.gov.au/news/linda-teggs-grasslands-opens/

5-9 Park[ing] Day, Seattle, SDOT Photos (CC): https://www.flickr.com/photos/sdot_photos/37311920225

5-10 Trash Bash, Seattle (2008) by John Cornicello

5-11 Melbourne stormwater sign courtesy of i-SUSTAIN

5-12 Puget Sound Starts Here by Nancy Rivenburgh

5-13 Old Cemetery Biodiversity sign, Longford, Ireland:
http://www.longfordleader.ie/gallery/features/273152/working-to-improve-the-environment-fantastic-proj-
ects-funded-in-county-longford.html

5-14 Walk Your City sign for San Jose CA, 2015 by Richard Masoner (CC):
https://www.flickr.com/photos/bike/17056977816

5-15 Bicycle counter in Copenhagen by James Cridland (CC): https://www.flickr.com/people/jamescridland/ [CC
BY 2.0 (https://creativecommons.org/licenses/by/2.0)], via Wikimedia Commons

5-16 Tempelhof Feld Kites:
https://www.berlin.de/senuvk/umwelt/stadtgruen/aktuelles/de/projekte/tempelhofer_feld/index.shtml

5-17 New Road Brighton: http://thisbigcity.net/five-ideas-from-brighton-for-socially-sustainable-cities/

5-18 Community Tree Planting, Yerevan, Armenia by Dfortuna (CC):
https://commons.wikimedia.org/wiki/File:Synopsys_Armenia_-_Tree_Planting_in_Yerevan.jpg

5-19 Melbourne Bioblitz Promotional Poster: https://participate.melbourne.vic.gov.au/bioblitz

5-20 Participant in Community Character in a Box. Photographer unknown, in City of Austin project albums
https://www.flickr.com/photos/119725136@N06/14262832996

5-21 Bike symbol contest, Portland, PDOT photos: https://www.portlandoregon.gov/transportation/73492

5-22 Vote Your Butt: Twitter photo @hubbubUK Sept 3, 2015

5-23 Immigrant Woman and Bike in Copenhagen by Jim Mueller

5-24 I Got A Tune Up Logo courtesy of Billings, Montana Department of Neighborhoods

5-25 App recording pothole courtesy of Feet First

5-26 and 5-27 Make Sunday Special Road Signs, Bristol UK by George Ferguson

5-28 Farmer on Samsø Island wind turbine (2018) by Thinna Aniella

5-29 Brownsville Community Health Fair by Jason Hoekema for The Brownsville Herald
http://www.brownsvilleherald.com/news/local/article_9bdece9e-abc9-11e7-933b-2b4d11ff7c5f.html

5-30 Green Seattle Day tree planting by Jim Avery, Forterra

5-31 Growing sustainably project, San Jose: http://cucsj.org/projects/gs_garden/

5-32 Space to Brace art installation, Cape Farewell Project:
http://www.capefarewell.com/latest/projects/space-to-breathe.html

5-33 Roving Green Line, Minneapolis, Creative City Making Blog:
https://creativecitymaking.files.wordpress.com/2013/07/2013-07-15-21-42-34.jpg

5-34 City of Color mural, The Patch Project:
https://thepatchproject.com/projects/city-of-color-public-art-murals-hoarding-monica-wickeler/

5-35 Postcard Project: http://www.hunterfranks.com/#/neighborhood-postcard-project/

5-36 One Tree per Child by George Ferguson

Chapter 6: Moving People

6-1 Second Avenue, Seattle Photo Shoot, Cars (2008) courtesy of i-SUSTAIN and Maximage

6-2 Second Avenue, Seattle, Photo Shoot, People in Car Configuration (2008) courtesy of i-SUSTAIN and Maximage

6-3 Second Avenue, Seattle, Photo Shoot, People on Light Rail (2008) courtesy of i-SUSTAIN and Maximage

6-4 Walking school bus in Stretford, England (2013) by University of Salford Press (CC): https://www.flickr.com/photos/salforduniversity/10208723123/

6-5 Pedestrian priority street, Istanbul, Turkey (2011) by wnhsl (CC): https://www.flickr.com/photos/wneuheisel/6376451065

6-6 Charlottesville, Virginia Downtown Mall (2010) by abi.bhattachan (CC): https://www.flickr.com/photos/abibhattachan/4757897339

6-7 The Tianzifang neighborhood, Shanghai, China (2010) by Michael Vito (CC): https://www.flickr.com/photos/michaelvito/8223148732

6-8 Neighborhood demolition in Shanghai, China (2008) by i-SUSTAIN

6-9 Corredor Madero, Mexico City, Mexico (2012) by iivangm (CC): https://www.flickr.com/photos/ivangm/7111435641

6-10 Ben Yehuda Street by day, Jerusalem, Israel (2007) by Yoninah [CC BY-SA 3.0 (https://creativecommons.org/licenses/by-sa/3.0) or GFDL (http://www.gnu.org/copyleft/fdl.html)], from Wikimedia Commons

6-11 Pedestrian sign, New South Wales, Australia (2009) by Amanda Slater (originally posted to Flickr as Parkes NSW) [CC BY-SA 2.0 (https://creativecommons.org/licenses/by-sa/2.0)], via Wikimedia Commons

6-12 Solar charging bench in D.C. courtesy of i-SUSTAIN

6-13 Crosswalk countdown timer by TCC: https://products.currentbyge.com/transportation-lighting/led-traffic-signals/pedestrian-signals - gallery-1

6-14 Brumman Netherlands Lighted Zebra Crossing by Lighted Zebra Crossing B.V.

6-15 Madrid Funnycross by Rafael Pérez Martinez (CC)

6-16 3-D crossing by Linda Bjork: https://www.instagram.com/p/BZT3M9THvkR/?utm_source=ig_embed

6-17 Cebritas, La Paz Bolivia by EEJCC (Own work) [CC BY-SA 4.0 (https://creativecommons.org/licenses/by-sa/4.0)], via Wikimedia Commons

6-18 Pedestrian ramp, Stockholm, Sweden (2014) by Johan Pontén

6-19 Traffic Light, Vienna, Austria courtesy of i-SUSTAIN

6-20 Berlin Ampelmann by Loozrboy (CC): https://www.flickr.com/photos/loozrboy/5321470272

6-21 Pedestrian Counting System, Melbourne, Australia by City of Melbourne: http://www.pedestrian.melbourne.vic.gov.au/ - date=21-08-2018&time=2

6-22 Walkscore for San Francisco, California (2015)

6-23 Bicycle training, Odense, Denmark by Cycling Embassy of Denmark: http://www.cycling-embassy.dk/2016/09/14/denmark-kids-bicycling-school-first-day/

6-24 Graph Copenhagen 1970-2016:
http://www.cycling-embassy.dk/2017/06/01/new-figures-cycling-copenhagen-break-record/

6-25 Bike path street cleaner, Copenhagen, Denmark by John Mauro (2012)

6-26 Biking on a snowy Day, Copenhagen, Denmark courtesy of i-SUSTAIN

6-27 Copenhagen blue intersections by Jim Mueller

6-28 Bicyclist on the pedestrian street in Copenhagen, Denmark by Jim Mueller

6-29 Bicycle signals in Copenhagen, Denmark by Michael Bo Rasmussen

6-30 The Copenhagen Bicycle Snake by Visit Copenhagen

6-31 2 Parking spaces, 20 Bicycles in Copenhagen, Denmark by Michael Bo Rasmussen

6-32 Bike parking Copenhagen, Denmark by Grey Geezer (CC):
https://commons.wikimedia.org/wiki/File:Bicycle_Parking_Copenhagen.jpg

6-33 Bike, baby and the dog, Copenhagen, Denmark by Michael Bo Rasmussen

6-34 Biking with Dad, Copenhagen, Denmark by Michael Bo Rasmussen

6-35 Bike Share Paris, France (2007) (CC): https://commons.wikimedia.org/wiki/File:Vélib%27_1,_Paris_
July_16,_2007.jpg

6-36 DC Bike Share (2010) by Kevin Kovaleski DDOT DC (CC):
http://www.flickr.com/photos/ddotphotos/4999689212/in/set-72157624852672085/

6-37 NYC Bike Share (2014) by Edward H. Blake (CC): https://www.flickr.com/photos/eblake/14752624240

6-38 Hangzhou, China Bike Share (2010) by Bradley Schroeder (CC):
https://www.flickr.com/photos/bradley_schroeder/9348103349

6-39 Ecobici Bike Share Map for Mexico City: https://www.ecobici.cdmx.gob.mx/en/stations-map

6-40 Toyko Bike Parking Lot Entrance courtesy of i-SUSTAIN

6-41 Robotic Underground Bicyle Parking in Japan by JFE Engineering Corp.:
http://www.jfe-eng.co.jp/en/products/machine/multi/mul01.html

6-42 Bicycle gutter in Copenhagen by Michael Bo Rasmussen

6-43 Bicycle gutter in parking garage in Tokyo, Japan (2013) courtesy of i-SUSTAIN

6-44 Bicycle escalator, Tokyo, Japan by Steven-L-Johnson (CC):
https://www.flickr.com/photos/stevenljohnson/14197338236/

6-45 Bikes on trains, Puget Sound (2006) by Oran Viriyincy (CC):
https://commons.wikimedia.org/wiki/File:Lower_floor_of_a_bi-level_Sound_Transit_commuter_train.jpg

6-46 Bike on bus, Seattle,Washington by Chris Hamby (CC):
https://www.flickr.com/photos/chrishamby/17100820838/

6-47 Bike service station, Washington, DC (2010) by MoBikeFed (CC):
https://www.flickr.com/photos/mobikefed/4427447140/

6-48 Library bicycle repair station courtesy of King County

6-49 Metrocable, Medellin, Colombia by Jorge Gobbi (CC):
https://www.flickr.com/photos/morrissey/10965169976/

6-50 BRT stop in Curitiba, Brazil by Jim Mueller

6-51 Transit Oriented Development (TOD), Curitiba, Brazil (2006) by Jim Mueller

6-52 Tram Rapid Transit in Istanbul, Turkey (2010) by Jim Mueller

6-53 Contemporary Melbourne Tram by Bernard Spragg (CC):
https://www.flickr.com/photos/volvob12b/26319555038/

6-54 Historic Melbourne Tram by eGuide Travel (CC)
https://www.flickr.com/photos/eguidetravel/5393361625

6-55 Colectivo, San Cristobal de las Casas, Mexico courtesy of i-SUSTAIN

6-56 Water Taxi, Victoria, British Columbia, Canada by Kasey Eriksen (CC):
https://www.flickr.com/photos/kaseyeriksen/16809215085/

6-57 Trailhead Direct van, Seattle courtesy of King County

Chapter 7: Supporting People

7-1 Vivero Alamar Urban Farm, Havana, Cuba (2013) by Nils Aguilar: http://voicesoftransition.org
https://commons.wikimedia.org/wiki/File:Voices_of_Transition_Mitglieder_Cooperativa_Alamar.png

7-2 Picardo Family P Patch, Seattle by Nancy Rivenburgh

7-3 Ample Harvest.org website (2018): http://ampleharvest.org/

7-4 Curitiba Garbage that is not Garbage, Curitiba, Brazil (2006) by Jim Mueller

7-5 Green Exchange programs, Curitiba, Brazil (2006) by Jim Mueller

7-6 Beacon Hill Food Forest volunteers: Beaconhillfoodforest.org

7-7 Backyard Chickens, Seattle, Washington (2010) by furtwangl (CC):
https://www.flickr.com/photos/furtwangl/4339138950/in/album-72157617242650652/

7-8 Rooftop bees in Melbourne, Australia by Melbourne City Rooftop Honey

7-9 Price History of Silicon PV Cells by Bloomberg New Energy Finance & pv.energytrend.com (CC):
https://commons.wikimedia.org/wiki/File:Price_history_of_silicon_PV_cells_since_1977.svg

7-10 PS10 Solar Towers, Seville Spain (2012) by Ron Huden

7-11 Crescent Dunes Solar Energy Project, Tonopah, Nevada (2014) by Amble (CC): http://commons.wikimedia.org/wiki/File: Crescent_Dunes_Solar_December_2014.JPG#filelinks

7-12 Rooftop Solar, Freiburg, Germany (2009) by Andrew Glaser (CC): http://commons.wikimedia.org/wiki/File:SoSie+SoSchiff_Ansicht.jpg

7-13 Big Belly Trash Bin, Edinburgh, Scotland by MJ Richardson (CC): http://www.geograph.org.uk/photo/2615687

7-14 Transporting Wind Turbines (2008) by Paul Anderson (CC): http://www.geograph.org.uk/photo/824546

7-15 Wind Turbines in the Harbor, Copenhagen, Denmark (2004) by Jim Mueller

7-16 Global Installed Wind Capacity (Data: GWEC): http://www.gwec.net/wp-content/uploads/2012/06/Global-Cumulative-Installed-Wind-Capacity-2001-2017.jpg

7-17 Green Wall Universidad del Claustro de Sor Juana, Mexico City, Mexico (2012) by Thelmadatter (CC): http://commons.wikimedia.org/wiki/File:GreenWallUCSJ01.JPG

7-18 Close-up of Green Wall, Mexico City, Mexico (2012) by Thelmadatter (CC): http://commons.wikimedia.org/wiki/File:GreenWallUCSJ01.JPG

7-19 Council House II Building, Melbourne, Australia (2007) courtesy of i-SUSTAIN

7-20 The Nykredit Building on a Cloudy Day, Copenhagen, Denmark (2012) by John Mauro

7-21 The Nykredit Building on a Sunny Day, Copenhagen, Denmark (2012) courtesy of i-SUSTAIN

7-22 The Nykredit Building Window Screens, Copenhagen, Denmark (2012) by Michael Bo Rasmussen

7-23 Wind Towers, Yazd, Iran (2008) by Julia Maudlin (CC): http://commons.wikimedia.org/wiki/File:Tower_of_Silence_Wind_Towers_and_Ice_Chamber_Yazd_Iran.jpg

7-24 Zion National Park, Utah: http://www.zionnationalpark.com/explore/things-to-see/museums-visitors-centers/

7-25 Low Cost Green Roof, Malmö, Sweden (2004) by Jim Mueller

7-26 8 House Green Roofs, Copenhagen, Denmark (2012) by Michael Bo Rasmussen

7-27 Green roofs, Berlin Germany (2006) by Denise Fong

7-28 Permeable Pavement, Malmö Sweden (2012) by Michael Bo Rasmussen

7-29 Tramway, Nantes, France (2012) by Ingolf BLN (CC): http://en.wikipedia.org/wiki/File:Flickr_-_IngolfBLN_-_Nantes_-_Tramway_-_Ligne_3_-_Orvault_%2817%29.jpg

7-30 Belltown Stormwater Drainage, Seattle, Washington (2016) by Dongho Chang courtesy of SDOT: https://www.flickr.com/photos/sdot_photos/25004323191/

7-31 Parque Tanguá, Curitiba, Brazil (2007) by Leonardo Stabile (CC): http://commons.wikimedia.org/wiki/File:Parque_Tanguá_Curitiba.jpg

7-32 Rabalderparken, Roskilde Denmark (2013) by Rune Johansen; permission granted by SNE Architects

7-33 Western Harbor Canal, Malmö, Sweden (2004) by Jim Mueller

7-34 Western Harbor Drain, Malmö, Sweden (2004) by Denise Fong

7-35 Augustenborg Natural Drainage, Malmö (2006) by Jorchr (CC):
http://commons.wikimedia.org/wiki/File:Augustenborg,_Malmö.jpg

7-36 Dockside Green, Victoria, B.C. courtesy of i-SUSTAIN

7-37 Tokyo Park courtesy of i-SUSTAIN

7-38 Tree Planting, Franklin Square, West Baltimore (2011) by Scott Kashnow for Friends of West Baltimore
(CC): https://www.flickr.com/photos/westbaltimoresquares/5840021735

7-39 Bosco Verticale, Milan, Italy (2014) by Nguyen Tan Tin (CC):
https://www.flickr.com/photos/126011099@N05/14805121310/

7-40 Kallang River Daylighting By Pagodashophouse. - Own work, CC BY-SA 3.0, https://commons.wikimedia.
org/w/index.php?curid=19065126

7-41 Pollinator Project Butterfly Crossing Sign, Seattle (2009) by flickr user J (CC):
https://www.flickr.com/photos/jseattle/8211246568/

7-42 Pollinator Project Installation, Seattle (2009) by flickr user J (CC):
https://www.flickr.com/photos/jseattle/8210156875/

7-43 Girl and Tree, Melbourne (2009) by Tiffanie.J (CC):
https://www.flickr.com/photos/tjl-photography/5338003258/

7-44 and 7-45 Nature pop up play site and sign, Minneapolis, MN (2016) by Andrew Wilt

Photo Credits

About the Authors

Patricia Chase is an urban strategist and consultant. She works with developers, architects, local politicians, and city officials to expose them to global best practices in urban sustainability. Her company, i-SUSTAIN, leads professional research delegations to cities throughout the world.

Nancy K. Rivenburgh, Ph.D. is a professor at the University of Washington, Seattle, Washington. As a social scientist, her work investigates the ways in which communication, creativity, and community engagement can make cities more livable and sustainable.

Patricia Chase

Nancy Rivenburgh

Acknowledgments

The authors would like to thank the Department of Communication and the College of Arts and Sciences at the University of Washington for grants supporting this book project. This book would have never happened without the support of i-SUSTAIN's clients who travelled the world to learn about best practices in urban development with the goal of making their own cities better. These people—local politicians, executive city staff, real estate developers, architects and others—are among the most intelligent, creative and open-minded that Patricia is proud to know. We want to thank Jim Mueller and Ron Huden for providing excellent photos taken while participating in i-SUSTAIN delegations and Michael Bo Rasmussen for his outstanding photos. We also thank the many individuals and organizations who make their photos available, through permission or Creative Commons licenses, for audiences to enjoy, learn from, and use to vicariously travel the world. A big thanks to Quinn Rivenburgh for valuable, and meticulous, research assistance. A well-deserved, huge thanks to the Scan/Design Foundation for their ongoing support of learning from global best practices. Patricia would also like to honor her dear friend, Svend Auken (1943–2009), who was her greatest influence in trying to do her bit to make the world a little better. Svend, a Danish politician, dedicated his life to public service. His leadership, friendship, kindness, and sense of humor are missed daily. Finally, we are grateful to all the individuals and organizations, public and private, around the world who bring such passion and energy to making cities more livable and sustainable. It is through their tireless and creative efforts, some highlighted in this book, that cities can become the solution to, and no longer the cause of, the environmental and societal challenges we face.